150+
Easy Science
Experiments

COPYRIGHT © 1999 Mark Twain Media, Inc.

ISBN 1–58037–107–8

Printing No. CD–1334

Mark Twain Media, Inc., Publishers
Distributed by Carson-Dellosa Publishing Company, Inc.

Table of Contents

Introduction

The world of information is expanding at such an unbelievable rate due to technology. Satellites allow instant communication between every nook and cranny throughout the world. Television coverage can be instantaneous, and computers, through the Internet, give access to millions of pieces of information, covering every conceivable subject.

Students living in this exploding age of technology are so fortunate that so much is available to them. However, this sometimes glut of information can completely overwhelm students, causing them to throw up their hands and become discouraged. This is where the teacher can help the learner focus on the basics.

This science experiments book is designed to enable the student to focus on basic science principles, which seem obvious to some students but are elusive to others. A structured approach to learning these principles is important to each individual.

Students need to develop the habit of looking at the world around them, using an organized approach to learning, and develop habits that will serve them well throughout their lives.

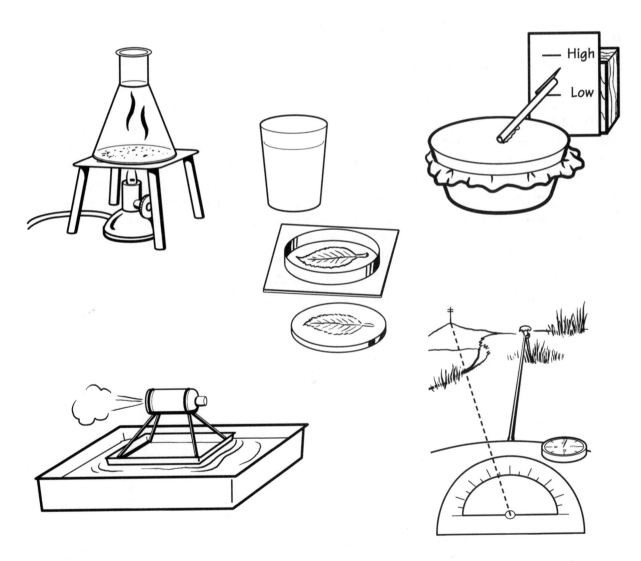

How to Use This Book

It is suggested that students develop the habit of looking at "things" in the world using a form of the "scientific method." We suggest that the student use the following steps to organize their experiments/demonstrations/projects. This is just one of the many forms of the "scientific method." Possible steps are as follows:

1. Ask a question.

2. Review what is known about the topic.

3. Formulate a hypothesis.

4. Experiment to test the hypothesis.

5. Observe the experiment; record and organize the results.

6. Analyze the results and draw conclusions.

7. Share the results with others.

Each activity may be completed as an individual student experiment, demonstration, or project, or activities may be completed by student teams. Activities may also be done as total class experiments, demonstrations, or projects. Some of the activities might be best done by teacher demonstration. Choice of method many times will depend on lab facilities, availability of equipment and supplies, time, and most importantly, student safety.

Regardless of whether the activity is conducted as an experiment or demonstration, the student will need to follow the steps of an identified scientific method. We have provided a suggested method that may be modified to fit your classroom needs.

It is suggested that you duplicate and make readily available to your students a supply of the Experiment/Demonstration Forms found on pages 5–7 of this book. Students may then add the completed Experiment/Demonstration Forms to their ongoing science journals.

Sample Experiment/Demonstration Form

Question:

How can we prove that air exerts pressure?

Review What Is Known About the Question:

Obtain information about this topic in the library and on the Internet.

Formulate a Hypothesis:

"Air pressure is due to the weight of the air above us."

Experiment/Demonstration to Test Your Hypothesis:

Step 1: Place a hard-boiled egg (shell removed) on the opening of an empty glass orange or fruit juice container with an opening in the jar of approximately $1\frac{1}{2}$ inches in diameter. What happens? (Record observations.)

The egg cannot be pushed through the bottle without exerting force.

Step 2: Remove the egg and insert a flaming torch made from a piece of rolled up paper into the glass container. What happens? (Record observations.)

The paper burns in the bottle.

Step 3: Quickly place the egg back on top of the bottle. What happens? (Record observations.)

The paper burns until the oxygen in the bottle is used up and the egg is sucked into the jar.

Step 4: _____

_____

_____

Repeat the Experiment if Necessary for Further Data:

_____

_____

_____

_____

_____

_____

Analyze Results and Draw Conclusions:

The flame uses up most of the oxygen in the bottle. Since there is less pressure pushing upward and more pressure pushing downward, the egg is literally "pushed" into the bottle. This demonstrates that the air outside the bottle does exert pressure.

_____

_____

_____

_____

_____

_____

_____

Share the Results With Others and Add This Information to Your Science Journal

Name _____ Date _____

Experiment/Demonstration #_____

Question:

_____

_____

_____

Review What Is Known About the Question:

_____

_____

_____

_____

_____

_____

Formulate a Hypothesis:

_____

_____

_____

Experiment/Demonstration to Test Your Hypothesis:

Step 1: _____

_____

_____

_____

_____

Step 2: _____

_____

_____

_____

_____

Step 3: _____

_____

_____

_____

_____

Step 4: _____

_____

_____

_____

_____

Repeat the Experiment if Necessary for Further Data:

_____

_____

_____

_____

_____

_____

_____

_____

Analyze Results and Draw Conclusions:

_____

_____

_____

_____

_____

_____

_____

_____

_____

_____

_____

_____

_____

_____

_____

_____

_____

_____

Share the Results With Others and Add This Information to Your Science Journal

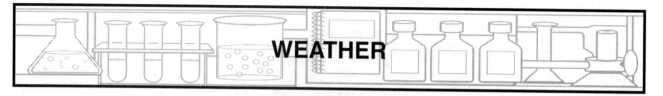

WEATHER

Weather is, in reality, the study of the air, since the condition of the air is what determines the weather. When air bubbles move through water, most people think of bubbles in the water rather than bubbles of air. The belief that heat tends to rise indicates that air is not commonly thought of as a real substance. The comment that it is a warm day or a cold day shows a general lack of awareness that it is really the air that is warm or cold.

Though we live our whole lives at the bottom of an ocean of air, the concept that air has weight seems a difficult one to grasp. The understanding that atmospheric pressure is due to the weight of the air above us also seems difficult. These facts are not really perplexing when we remember that, even up until the sixteenth century, no one had yet interpreted air pressure phenomena correctly.

We need clear understandings about air based on real experience. These important understandings cannot be developed by means of the usual limited number of formalized demonstrations followed by rehearsed generalizations.

Weather changes from day to day and even from hour to hour. Lets take a look at several factors that determine the weather and ask ourselves the following questions.

- How do we know that air exerts pressure?
- How does heating and cooling affect materials?
- How does heat travel from one place to another?
- What effect does water have on weather conditions?
- How do air masses and fronts affect the weather?
- What are some causes of weather changes?

How Do We Know That Air Exerts Pressure?

Experiment/Demonstration #1

Procedure:

Place a hard-boiled egg (shell removed) on top of an empty orange or fruit juice bottle with an opening in the jar of approximately $1\frac{1}{2}$ inches in diameter. The egg cannot be pushed through the bottle without exerting force. Remove the egg and insert a flaming torch made from a piece of rolled-up paper into the bottle. Quickly place the egg back on top of the bottle. What happens?

Materials Needed:

Hard-boiled Egg
Matches or Lighter
Orange or Fruit Juice Bottle
Rolled-up Sheet of Paper

Experiment/Demonstration #2

Procedure:

Obtain a discarded rectangular gallon metal can with a cap (varnish, wax, or syrup can) and pump out the air with a vacuum pump. Observe what happens.

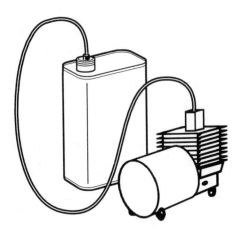

Materials Needed:

One-gallon Rectangular Metal Can With Cap
Vacuum Pump

Experiment/Demonstration #3

Procedure:

Obtain a discarded rectangular gallon metal can with cap (varnish, wax, or syrup can) and put a small amount of water into the can. Heat the water with a hot plate or Bunsen burner until steam comes out of the opening in the top of the can. Quickly remove the can from the heat and put the cap tightly on the opening of the can. Set the can aside and watch it.

Materials Needed:

One-gallon Rectangular Metal Can With Cap
Water
Hot Plate or Bunsen Burner

Experiment/Demonstration #4

Procedure:

Fill a glass to the top with water. Place a card on the top of the glass larger than the diameter of the glass. Holding the card firmly on the glass, quickly turn the glass over. Remove your hand from the card carefully. What happens?

Caution: Perform this experiment over a pail or similar container.

Materials Needed:

Drinking Glass   Water
Paper Card   Pail

Experiment/Demonstration #5

Procedure:

In a deep dish or jar full of water, submerge a clear tumbler and allow it to fill with water. Turn it to an inverted position and lift it straight up until nearly all of the glass is above the surface of the water in the jar. Observe what happens.

Materials Needed:

Deep Dish or Jar
Water
Tumbler (Small Glass)

Experiment/Demonstration #6

Procedure:

Obtain two plumber's force cups (plungers) and wet the bottom rim of each cup. (Two suction cups of equal size may be used instead.) Press the cups together to expel the air inside the cups. What happens when you try to pull them apart?

Materials Needed:

Two Plumber's Force Cups (Plungers) or
Two Suction Cups

Experiment/Demonstration #7

Procedure:

Make a nail hole near the bottom of a small-sized can. Fill the can with water. Hold the palm of your hand tightly over the top of the can. What happens? Lift your hand. What happens?

Materials Needed:

Small Tin Can   Water
Nail   Hammer

Experiment/Demonstration #8

Procedure:

Punch holes in an empty milk carton and note it will sink to the bottom of the tank of water. Attach the balloon to the tubing and place this arrangement in the end of the milk carton. Blow up the balloon. What happens?

Materials Needed:

Quart Milk Carton (empty)
Two Feet of Rubber Tubing
One Large Balloon
Tank of Water

What Are Some of the Uses of Air Pressure?

Experiment/Demonstration #9

Procedure:

   Place a drinking straw in a full bottle of water. Press clay around the neck to close the opening between the straw and the bottle. Hold the clay tightly to the bottle with your fingers and try to drink through the straw. What happens?

Materials Needed:

Empty Soda Bottle   Drinking Straw
Clay   Water

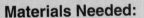

Experiment/Demonstration #10

Procedure:

   Insert a glass tube into a one-hole stopper. Insert the stopper into a soda bottle completely filled with water. Suck on the tube and try to get a drink of water. Then loosen the stopper and try to take another drink of water. What happens?

Materials Needed:

Glass Tube   One-hole Stopper
Empty Soda Bottle   Water

Experiment/Demonstration #11

Procedure:

Press four or five lumps of clay over the rim of a glass jar. Fill the jar with water and set a dish in an inverted position on the lumps of clay. Now, with one hand on the dish and the other holding the jar, quickly invert both the dish and the jar. Use the dropper to remove some of the water in the dish. Watch for air bubbles to enter the jar as water is removed.

Bottles of drinking water are often inverted this way in office buildings.

Materials Needed:

Glass Jar   Water
Empty Dish (like a pie pan)   Clay

Experiment/Demonstration #12

Procedure:

Wet the bottom of a sink stopper and press it firmly against some flat surface such as the top of a stool or the bottom of a pail. Then pull upward on the surface of the stopper. What happens?

List some common devices that operate on this principle.

Materials Needed:

Sink Stopper   Stool or Pail
Water

Experiment/Demonstration #13

Procedure:

Use a medicine dropper to transfer water from one vessel to another. What happens? Why does it happen?

Materials Needed:

Medicine Dropper
Water
Two Bowls (or other vessels to hold liquid)

Experiment/Demonstration #14

Procedure:

Use a rubber tube as a siphon to transfer water from one vessel to another. Fill the rubber tube by placing it under water or by holding under a faucet. Pinch both ends and place them in separate vessels of water. Raise one vessel so that the water surface in it is above the water surface of the other vessel. When most of the water has been transferred from the first vessel, raise the second vessel.

CAUTION: Be prepared in case of spillage.

Materials Needed:

A Length of Rubber Tubing (depends on size of vessels and space of work area)
Two Bowls, Jars, Tanks
Water

15

How Can We Make a Simple Barometer?

Experiment/Demonstration #15

Procedure:

Stretch a piece of thin rubber over the mouth of a shallow can or jar. Tie string tightly around the top of the can or jar to hold the rubber piece in place. Glue a drinking straw on the piece of rubber so that one end of the straw is on the center of the rubber. Then fasten a small piece of toothpick or match in the other end of the straw to act as a pointer. Place the can or jar so that the pointer is not quite touching a piece of paper or cardboard that has been calibrated as "high" or "low." What happens?

Record your readings daily and discuss the operational principle of this improvised barometer.

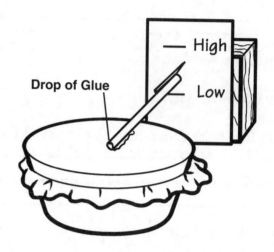

Drop of Glue — High — Low

Materials Needed:

Shallow Jar or Can
Sheet of Rubber (size depends on size of jar or can)
String or Rubber Bands
Glue (that will hold plastic to rubber)
Drinking Straw
Wood Splint (toothpick or match)
Cardboard (calibrated to "high" and "low")
Small Block of Wood (or something to keep cardboard upright)

Experiment/Demonstration #16

Procedure:

   Make a thermos-bottle barometer as shown in the diagram. Pour some colored water into the bent glass tubing and note the effect on the liquid as the pressure changes from day to day. Discuss the reason for using a thermos bottle rather than an uninsulated bottle. Discuss the limitations of this type of barometer.

   Variations in atmospheric pressure are the least noticeable of the changes in air conditions. Collect evidence that changes in atmospheric pressure accompany weather changes.

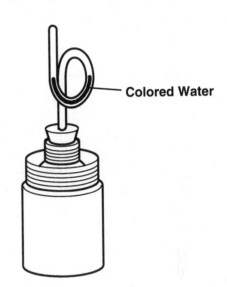

Colored Water

Materials Needed:

Bent Glass Tubing   Water
Food Coloring   Thermos Bottle

Experiment/Demonstration #17

Procedure:

   The "soda-bottle" barometer shown in the diagram will indicate changes in pressure only if it is kept at a uniform temperature. If the temperature is allowed to vary, it will operate on the same principle as a thermometer. Discuss the reasons for this.

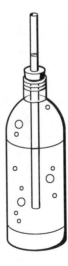

Materials Needed:

Soda Bottle (Empty)   Water
Drinking Straw (or Glass Tube)
One-hole Stopper

How Is a Barometer Used?

Experiment/Demonstration #18

Procedure:

If there are differences in elevation on or near the school grounds, it will be interesting to take barometric readings at the highest and lowest points.

It is also interesting to take a barometer along on a field trip. It may be possible to encounter multiple barometric readings throughout the trip, especially if the trip involves climbing hills.

A finely calibrated barometer will show a difference when readings are taken in the basement and on the top floor of the school building.

Record the reading of the barometer each place for several days. Make a graph of the daily pressure changes over that same period to relate the pressure changes to weather changes.

After keeping barometric pressure readings for several days, an understanding of the reasons for the variations should develop. Also point out that there are great waves in the atmosphere just as there are waves in the ocean. There are also great air currents similar in some ways to ocean currents.

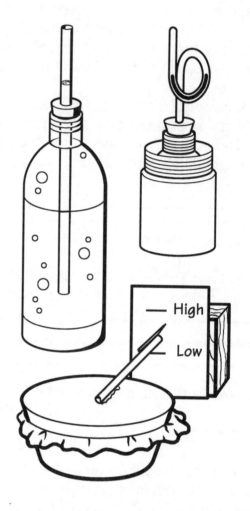

Materials Needed:

Barometers made in previous experiments:
    Simple Barometer
    Thermos-bottle Barometer
    "Soda-bottle" Barometer

How Does Heating and Cooling Affect a Solid?

Experiment/Demonstration #19

Procedure:

Locate an expansion ball and ring. First cool the ring and try to fit the ball through the ring. Then heat the ring and try to fit the ball through. What happens? Why?

Materials Needed:

Expansion Ball and Ring
Ice Pack (or Cool Source)
Heating Pad (or Heat Source)

Experiment/Demonstration #20

Procedure:

Tie a weight to a length of copper wire. Hang the wire from a support and allow it to swing freely, approximately $\frac{1}{16}$ of an inch above a table top. Swing the weight back and forth, then heat the wire with a candle or burner. Eventually the weight will touch the table and stop swinging. If the wire is allowed to cool, the weight will swing freely again. Why?

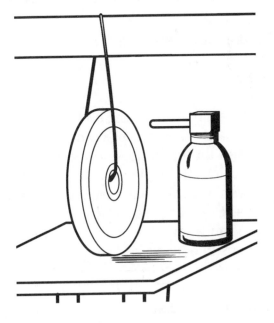

Materials Needed:

Small Weight
Length of Copper Wire
Support for Wire and Weight

Experiment/Demonstration #21

Procedure:

Suspend a length of copper wire horizontally between two supports. Hang a weight from the middle of the wire. Measure the distance from the end of the weight to the table top. Heat the horizontal copper wire with a burner. Now measure the distance from the end of the weight to the table top. What happened? Why?

As a variation, try using different types of metal wire and making a graph of your findings.

Materials Needed:

Two Supports	Burner
Small Weight	
Two Lengths of Copper Wire	

Experiment/Demonstration #22

Procedure:

Drive a nail near each end of a two-foot-long board. Fasten a piece of copper wire between the nails close to the board, and then fasten a bare piece of iron or steel wire between the two nails closer to the nail heads. (See illustration.) Hold the wires over a flame and move them back and forth. What happens to each wire? Why?

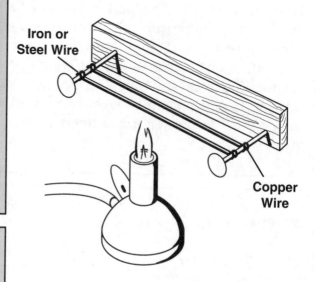

Iron or Steel Wire

Copper Wire

Materials Needed:

Board (two feet in length)	Burner
Four Nails	
Three Feet of Bare Copper Wire	
Three Feet of Bare Iron or Steel Wire	

What Happens to a Bimetallic Strip When it is Heated?

Experiment/Demonstration #23

Procedure:

Obtain a bimetal thermal strip consisting of a strip of brass and another of steel riveted closely together. What happens when the strip is heated?

Materials Needed:

Bimetal Thermal Strip   Burner
Tongs (to hold the strip over the flame)

How Can We Demonstrate the Principle of the Thermostat?

Experiment/Demonstration #24

Procedure:

The principle of the type of thermostat used to regulate room temperature can be demonstrated very easily by means of the apparatus shown in the diagram. A bimetallic strip is clamped in horizontal position to a support. A wire attached to the bimetallic strip is placed in a circuit with batteries and a small lamp. The end of a wire leading from the lamp is attached to another support so that it touches the end of the bimetallic strip. Heating the bar with a candle causes it to bend upward and break the circuit. As soon as the bar cools, it bends downward again and completes the circuit. The lamp of course represents the motors that drive the furnace and circulators.

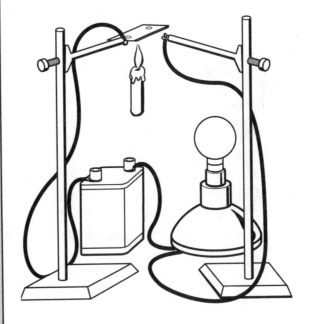

Materials Needed:

Bimetallic Strip   Batteries   Ringstand
Small Lamp   Wire   Candle

21

How Can We Make a Bimetallic Strip?

Experiment/Demonstration #25

Procedure:

Cut a strip of tin from a can and loop the ends of a bare copper wire over the ends of the strip of tin as shown in the diagram. Stretch the wire by inserting a shorter strip of metal bent into a V-shape. What happens when this is heated?
CAUTION: Clamp one end of the metal in position to prevent burns.

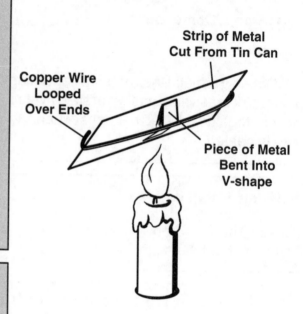

Materials Needed:

Tin Can   Bare Copper Wire
Burner or Candle Clamp

Why Are Sidewalks Laid in Sections of Concrete?

Experiment/Demonstration #26

Procedure:

Why are sidewalks laid in sections of concrete? Why are there new holes in roads and streets at the end of winter? Why should some air be let out of tires on hot summer days? Why is it easier to remove a metal lid from a jar if hot water is allowed to run over it?

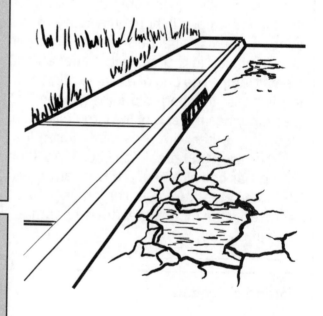

Materials Needed:

A trip outside to look at sidewalks and high-ways nearby. Pay close attention to the spaces between sections.

What Are Some Effects of Cooling and Heating Liquid?

Experiment/Demonstration #27

Procedure:

Put some colored water into a flask. Insert a long tube through a one-hole stopper to the bottom of the flask. The level of liquid can be adjusted by blowing in a bubble or releasing the stopper to let some air out. Warm and cool the flask. What happens?

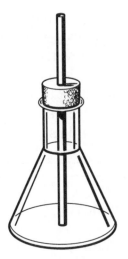

Materials Needed:

Flask   Water (food coloring)
One-hole Stopper   Long Glass Tube

What Are Some Effects of Cooling and Heating Air?

Experiment/Demonstration #28

Procedure:

Tie strings around the necks of two large flasks. Suspend the flasks from each end of a yard or meter stick. Suspend the center of the stick from a support as shown in the diagram, and balance the two flasks. Now heat one flask. What happens?

Materials Needed:

Two Large Flasks   Yard or Meter Stick
String   Burner
Support

Experiment/Demonstration #29

Procedure:

Wet the end of a long glass tube and fit it into a one-hole stopper. Insert the stopper into a glass flask. Invert this and immerse the lower end of the tube in a vessel of colored water. Heat the flask by holding it between the hands. What happens when the air in the flask warms and cools?

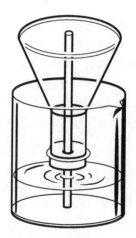

Materials Needed:

Long Glass Tube
Flask
One-hole Stopper
Large Beaker (or Vessel)
Food Coloring and Water

Experiment/Demonstration #30

Procedure:

Stretch a large empty balloon over the mouth of a flask. Place the flask on a stand over a burner and heat the flask. What happens?

Materials Needed:

Large Balloon
Large Flask
Burner
Stand

How Is Heat Transferred by Radiation?

Experiment/Demonstration #31

Procedure:

Fill with water a test tube that has its outside completely coated with black marker or tape. Fill a second clear test tube with water. Insert a thermometer into each and place both in a direct light source for 30 minutes. What happens to the temperature in each?

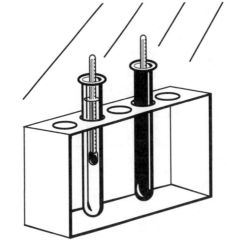

Materials Needed:

Two Test Tubes
Black Marker or Tape
Light Source (or Sun)

Water
Thermometers

Is Metal a Good Conductor of Heat?

Experiment/Demonstration #32

Procedure:

Suspend a copper wire between two supports 12 inches apart. Attach copper shot to the wire with wax placed 1 inch apart. Place a candle at one end of the copper wire, not directly under a copper shot. What happens as the wire heats up?

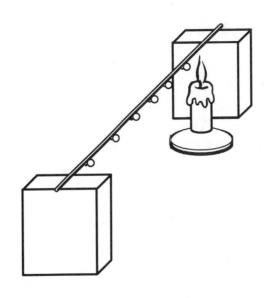

Materials Needed:

Length of Copper Wire
Six Copper Shots
Two Supports

Wax
Candle

Is Water a Poor Conductor of Heat?

Experiment/Demonstration #33

Procedure:

Incline a test tube filled with cold water and heat the top region. What happens to region A (top)? What happens to region B? What happens to the test tube? What does this experiment tell us about the conducting ability of water and glass?

Materials Needed:

Test Tube (labeled A on top and B on bottom)
Water   Burner
Apparatus to Hold Test Tube in an Inclined Position

Experiment/Demonstration #34

Procedure:

Hold a piece of ice in the bottom of a tilted test tube with a coil of solder wire. Heat the upper part of the test tube. What happens to the ice? What happens to the wire? What happens to the test tube?

Materials Needed:

Test Tube   Length of Solder Wire
Ice Cube   Burner

How Can We Demonstrate Convection Currents in a Liquid?

Experiment/Demonstration #35

Procedure:

Convection currents in water can be demonstrated by placing some particles of sawdust into a beaker of water. Heat the beaker over a burner. What happens?

Materials Needed:

Large Beaker
Burner
Sawdust
Water

Experiment/Demonstration #36

Procedure:

Equip a bottle with a two-hole stopper. Extend a glass tube out of the bottle and another to reach close to the bottom. Fill the bottle with hot water dyed with food coloring and then submerge it in a large beaker of cold water. What happens?

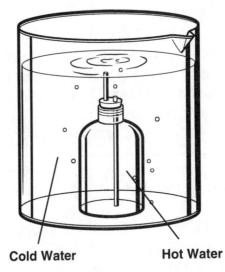

Cold Water   **Hot Water**

Materials Needed:

Bottle   Food Coloring
Two-hole Stopper   Large Beaker
Two Glass Tubes   Water

How Can We Demonstrate Convection Currents (Wind) in Air?

Experiment/Demonstration #37

Procedure:

The smoke box consists of two lamp chimneys or large glass tubes mounted above two openings in a box 12 x 12 x 20 cubic centimeters. When a lit candle is burned beneath one of the chimneys, and lit smoking paper is held over the other, the path of the convection currents are readily seen.

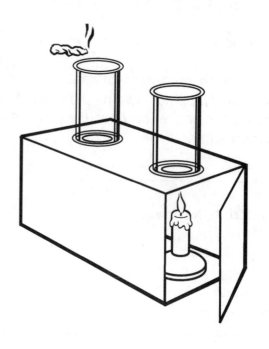

Materials Needed:

12 x 12 x 20 Cubic Centimeter Box
Large Glass Tubes or Lamp Chimneys
Candle
Smoking Touch Paper

Experiment/Demonstration #38

Procedure:

Lower a lit candle into a milk bottle or juice jar by means of a wire. Separate the hot and cold air currents by means of a cardboard strip as shown. Trace the air currents with smoking punk or smoke paper.

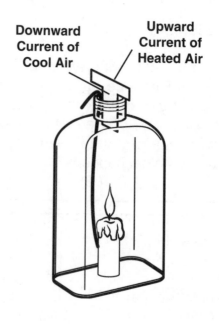

Downward Current of Cool Air

Upward Current of Heated Air

Materials Needed:

Juice Jar   Candle
Cardboard Strip   Wire
Smoking Punk or Smoke Paper

Experiment/Demonstration #39

Procedure:

Draw a spiral on a sheet of paper or light cardboard and if desired, draw a snake's head at the outer end. Cut out the spiral and suspend it by a thread tied to the inner end over a source of heat. What happens?

Materials Needed:

Paper
Scissors
String
Heat Source (e.g., candle)

Experiment/Demonstration #40

Procedure:

Cut out a metal can top with a rotary can opener so as to have a disc of metal. Punch a depression in the exact center. Make six or eight cuts along radial lines almost to the center and give each of the blades thus formed a twist in the same direction. Mount the wheel on a pointed wire and hold it over a candle or other source of heat. A carefully made wheel of this kind will also turn when held over a heat radiator or a lighted electric lamp.

Materials Needed:

Metal Can   Heat Source
Rotary Can Opener   Pointed Wire
An Adult to Help With Cutting Metal

How Can We Make a Simple Thermometer?

Experiment/Demonstration #41

Procedure:

Use the apparatus in the diagram to show how a thermometer works. Heat the flask over a burner or set it in the sunlight. Notice the rise in the water column in the tube. Cool the flask by placing it in cold water.

On the following day, when the water in the flask is the same temperature as the air in the room, make a mark on the white card taped to the tube, at the water level in the tube. Opposite this mark indicate the room temperature as indicated by the classroom thermometer.

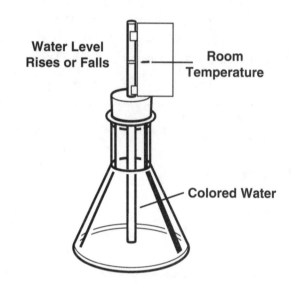

Water Level Rises or Falls

Room Temperature

Colored Water

Materials Needed:

Flask	One-hole Stopper
Water Tape	Tube Burner
Food Coloring	White Card

Experiment/Demonstration #42

Procedure:

A simple air thermometer like the one in the diagram illustrates the relatively greater expansion and contraction of gases with changes in temperature as compared to liquids. Heat the flask gently with the palms of the hands to drive out air bubbles, then let the bottle cool. What happens?

Check the level of the water in the glass tube after the flask has been heated.

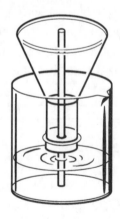

Materials Needed:

Flask	Small Beaker
Ring Stand	Glass Tube
Food Coloring	Water

How Can We Make a Simple Weather Vane?

Experiment/Demonstration #43

Procedure:

A very sensitive weather vane can be made from very common and easy to find household objects. Insert the feather in the end of the straw and push a pin through the straw into the pencil eraser at the balancing point.

Materials Needed:

Pencil	Pin
Drinking Straw	Feather

Experiment/Demonstration #44

Procedure:

Make thin wood or metal "arrows" and "feather" as shown in the sketch. Fasten these to a strip of wood. Balance the arrangement on a knife edge and drill a vertical hole at the place where it balances. Drive a nail vertically in the center of a dowel rod or end of an upright stick, and mount the other end of the dowel rod or the stick onto the center of the wooden base. Indicate the four directions on the base. Set the weather vane outside with the directions on the base facing actual North, etc. Do not place the weather vane too close to a building.

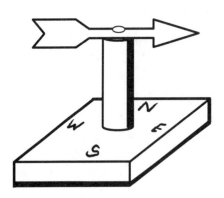

Materials Needed:

Wood or Metal "Arrows"	Dowel Rod or Stick
Wooden Base	Nail & Hammer

How Can We Make a Simple Anemometer?

Experiment/Demonstration #45

Procedure:

Cut a 10-centimeter slit in the side of each paper cup. Mark one paper cup with an "X" using a dark marker. Find the center of each 10 x 30 cm piece of cardboard. Overlap the two strips to form a cross, matching the centers. Tape the two strips together. Slide each end of the crossed strips through the slit in one of the cups. (Be sure all cups face the same direction.) Carefully put the small nail through the center of the two strips. Roll the 45 x 4 cm piece of cardboard into a long tube no larger than one centimeter in diameter. Place one end of the tube in the empty milk jug or carton. Carefully add sand to the jug or carton until the tube is able to stand upright freely. Place the crossed strips over the tube, putting the nail in the center of the tube.

Materials Needed:

Four Paper Cups
One Small Nail
Pencil
Markers
Sand
Scissors
Tape
One Empty Milk Jug or Carton
Two 10-centimeter x 30-centimeter strips of
    cardboard
One 45-centimeter x 4-centimeter strip of
    thin cardboard

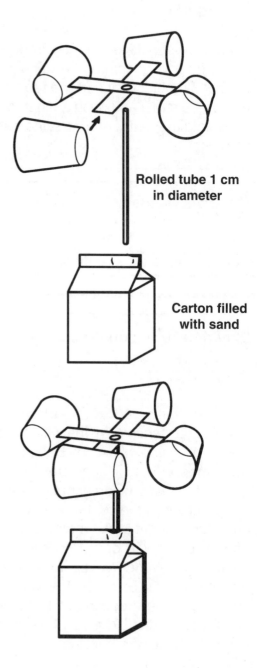

Rolled tube 1 cm
in diameter

Carton filled
with sand

What Effect Does Water Have on Weather Conditions?

Experiment/Demonstration #46

Demonstrate in various ways that water is constantly evaporating into the air. Invert a jar over a potted plant, breathe on the window, or wash the chalkboard and watch the film of water disappear.

In discussing evaporation, it is interesting to note that when the relative humidity in an average-size classroom is 100 percent, the air will contain about 3000 ml of water. Measure out 3 liters of water to demonstrate how much that is.

Experiment/Demonstration #47

Procedure:

Dip a cloth in water. Wring out the cloth and place it on a hanger. Hook the clothes hanger on one end of a long stick. Balance the stick by tying something of equal weight to the wet cloth on the other end of the stick. What happens as the water evaporates?

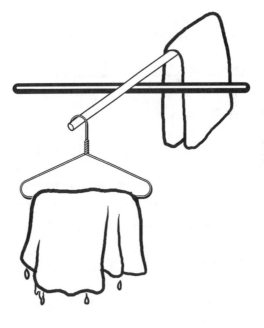

Materials Needed:

Piece of Cloth
Water
Long Stick
Hanger
String
Weight

33

Experiment/Demonstration #48

Procedure:

Place a flower pot full of moist soil on one platform of a beam balance. Balance it with weights on the other platform. What happens to the weight of the flower pot over the next few days?

Materials Needed:

Flower Pot   Moist Soil
Beam Balance   Weights

Experiment/Demonstration #49

Procedure:

Tie plastic wrap around a leaf of a houseplant. What happens inside the plastic wrap?

Materials Needed:

Plastic Wrap   House Plant

Experiment/Demonstration #50

Procedure:

Put ice and water in a metal can. What happens to the closed metal can?

Materials Needed:

Ice Water   Metal Can

Experiment/Demonstration #51

Procedure:

Obtain a clean dry flask and put it in a cold place. Blow into the cold flask through a glass tube until a film of moisture forms on the inside. Then stopper the flask tightly and warm it very gently. What happens to the film of moisture? What happens if you place the flask back in a cool place after that?

Materials Needed:

Flask   Gentle Heat Source
Stopper   Gentle Cool Source
Glass Tube

What Are Some Reasons for Changes in the Rate of Evaporation?

Experiment/Demonstration #52

Procedure:

Measure out 50 milliliters of water with a graduated cylinder and pour it into a vessel of much larger diameter. Again measure 50 milliliters in the graduated cylinder and allow it to remain within the cylinder. How much water has evaporated from each after 24 hours? Why?

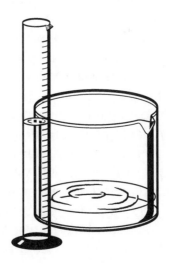

Materials Needed:

Water
Graduated Cylinder
Large Container (e.g., Large Beaker)

35

Experiment/Demonstration #53

Procedure:

Put equal amounts of water into two similar vessels. Set one vessel in the coolest place in the room and the other in the warmest place. What happens to the water levels by the next day? Why?

Materials Needed:

Two Similar Vessels   Graduated Cylinder
Water

Do Some Solids Evaporate Directly From a Solid to a Gas?

Experiment/Demonstration #54

Procedure:

Expose a small piece of dry ice to the air until it disappears. Place another small piece in a glass of water and watch the escape of the bubbles of carbon dioxide. This is an example of the evaporation of solids, which is generally not as well known as the evaporation of liquids.

An interesting mechanical effect may be shown by placing the bowl of a spoon on a piece of dry ice with the spoon handle lying on the desk or table. A high-pitched sound will be noted as the gas escapes.

Camphor, mothballs, iodine crystals, and other substances will also evaporate. This is additional evidence that they are made up of tiny invisible particles, which are in constant motion.

Materials Needed:

Dry Ice   Spoon   Glass of Water

What Effect Does Evaporation Have on Temperature?

Experiment/Demonstration #55

Procedure:

Moisten the back of the hand with a little rubbing alcohol. What happens to the alcohol? What happens to the temperature of the hand?

Materials Needed:

Rubbing Alcohol   A Hand

What Do We Mean by Relative Humidity?

Experiment/Demonstration #56

Procedure:

To understand relative humidity, compare the air to a sponge. Weigh a completely dry sponge on a spring scale suspended from a ring stand. Remove the sponge and add water until the sponge is soaked but not dripping. Weigh the sponge again and compute the weight of the amount of water that was added. The sponge is saturated. That is, it contains 100 % of the moisture it is capable of holding.

Thoroughly dry the sponge. This time add one-half or one-fourth of the known amount of water the sponge will hold. It can now be said that the sponge (which represents the air) is 50 % or 25 % saturated.

If more than the known amount of water is added to the sponge, the excess water will drop out of the sponge, and the sponge is now supersaturated.

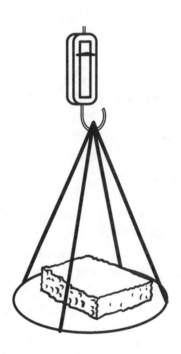

Materials Needed:

Sponge   Scale   Water   Ring Stand

37

How Can We Determine the Dew Point of the Air?

Experiment/Demonstration #57

Procedure:

Determine the dew point of the air by slowly adding cracked ice to water in a polished can. At what temperature does moisture first form on the outside of the can as the mixture is stirred?

Materials Needed:

Cracked Ice   Water
Polished Can   Thermometer

What Is the Water Cycle?

Experiment/Demonstration #58

Procedure:

Heat some water until it is near the boiling point. Pour the hot water into a drinking glass until it is about two-thirds full, and rotate the glass so as to wet the sides all the way to the top. Now put some cold water into a Florence flask and set the flask on the glass at an angle as shown in the diagram.

Water will evaporate from the surface in the glass and condense on the cold flask. Drops of the condensed water will continue to fall back into the glass. This demonstration makes a simple approach to developing a concept of the water cycle. Evaporation, condensation, and precipitation continue inside the glass just as they do in the outside world.

Materials Needed:

Water   Drinking Glass   Pan
Hot Plate   Florence Flask

Experiment/Demonstration #59

Procedure:

Heat a container of water. Hold a cold plate over the boiling water. (Be careful not to pass your hand over the steam.) Eventually droplets of water will accumulate onto the cold plate. Collect the falling droplets in a jar. This demonstrates the principle of the water cycle. (Water rises, is cooled, and falls down as a form of precipitation.)

Experiment/Demonstration #60

Procedure:

Show how rain is formed by filling an aquarium half full of water. Cover it with a glass plate. Place the container by a sunny window. As the sun warms the water, some will evaporate and fill the air above with moisture. Some moisture will gather on the underside of the cool glass plate. When a sufficient amount of water has condensed, it will form into drops and will fall back into the bottom of the container like rain.

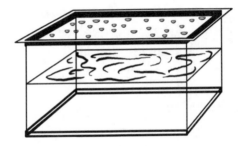

Experiment/Demonstration #61

Procedure:

Place a box of soil (with seedlings if possible) on a table. Place a metal tray about a foot above the box. Place cracked ice on top of the metal tray. Place a tea kettle or a flask containing water over a source of heat so that the steam will "spray" between the soil and the tray.

The tea kettle or flask serves as the earth's source of water. This evaporates and rises up to the cool tray, which represents the cold upper layers of air above the earth. Here the moisture condenses on the tray and drips back on the soil as rain.

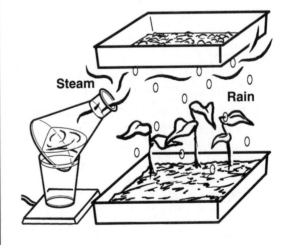

Steam

Rain

How Can We Make a Hygrometer?

Experiment/Demonstration #62

Procedure:

Make a hygrometer by mounting two similar thermometers vertically on a board. Tie one end of a piece of lamp wick around the bulb of one of the thermometers and immerse the other end of the wick in a small can or bottle of water. With a fan, circulate the air about the bulbs of the thermometers to induce faster evaporation and cooling of the wet bulb. When no further temperature change is noticed for the wet bulb, record the temperature readings of both the wet and dry bulb thermometers and check the chart to see what the relative humidity is.

Materials Needed:

Two Similar Thermometers
Bottle or Can of Water   Lamp Wick
Fan   Board

Dry Bulb	Difference Between Dry and Wet Bulb °F					
Temp.	3°	6°	9°	12°	15°	18°
°F	Relative Humidity (%)					
65°	85%	70%	56%	44%	31%	20%
70°	86%	72%	60%	48%	36%	26%
75°	87%	74%	62%	51%	40%	31%
80°	87%	75%	64%	54%	44%	35%

Experiment/Demonstration #63

Procedure:

Put a hygrometer in a large covered beaker that contains wet blotting paper. Warm the jar, then cool it. If the air is saturated, the wet and dry bulb readings should be the same at any temperature.

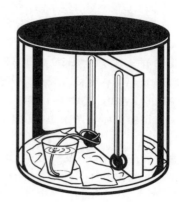

Materials Needed:

Hygrometer   Large Beaker
Wet Blotting Paper   Heat Source

Experiment/Demonstration #64

Procedure:

Make a hygrometer from a length of human hair. Soak a long length of hair in carbon tetrachloride to remove any oil and complete the hygrometer as shown in the diagram. Try the hygrometer outdoors and indoors on the same day. Keep it in the classroom and note any variations in the humidity from day to day.

Glue a paper pointer to the hair and then stretch the hair on the board and glue down each end. Check to see if the pointer moves toward the high or low marks.

Materials Needed:

Length of Hair   Glue
Carbon Tetrachloride   Pointer
Board

Experiment/Demonstration #65

Procedure:

Relate the principle of the hair hygrometer to the variation in lengths of clotheslines, tent ropes, and other fibers. Try setting up a rope hygrometer as shown in the diagram.

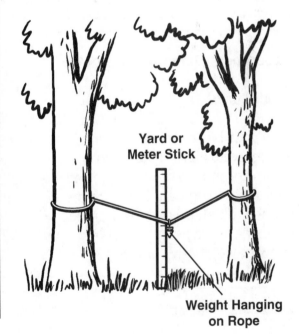

Yard or Meter Stick

Weight Hanging on Rope

Materials Needed:

Length of Rope
Yard/Meter Stick
Stake
Two Trees (somewhat close to each other)

How Can We Make a Chemical Hygrometer?

Experiment/Demonstration #66

Procedure:

Students are usually fascinated by color changes caused by the varying moisture content in the air. Dissolve 10 grams of cobalt chloride in 100 milliliters of water. Soak several strips of white cloth or filter paper in this solution. Remove them and allow them to dry. What happens if strips are placed indoors and outdoors?

Materials Needed:

10 Grams Cobalt Chloride
100 Milliliters Water
White Cloth or Filter Paper

How Many Inches of Snow Equal One Inch of Rain?

Experiment/Demonstration #67

Procedure:

If possible, obtain a column of snow from a recent snowfall. Measure the height of the column of snow in the juice can and then melt it in a matching can. Measure the depth of water and determine the difference. Repeat with different types of snow (e.g., dry, flaky snow or wet, heavy snow).

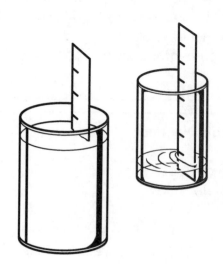

Materials Needed:

Snow   Ruler
Two Matching Juice Cans

How Can We Make a Simple Rain Gauge?

Experiment/Demonstration #68

Procedure:

If needed, ask an adult to help cut a large plastic bottle as seen in the diagram. Place thin strips of tape or marker on the bottle 10 millimeters apart. Place marbles or rocks in the bottom of the bottle for weight to stabilize the gauge. Pour water into the gauge up to the first mark or piece of tape. Record rainfall daily (each mark is 10 milliliters of rainfall). Dump the water and refill to the first mark at the end of the day to start over.

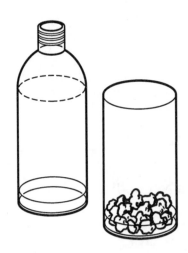

Materials Needed:

Large Plastic Bottle   Ruler
Marker or Tape   Water
Marbles or Rocks

How Can We Make Smog?

Experiment/Demonstration #69

Procedure:

Hold a lit match in the mouth of a glass jug. This will "seed" the air within the jug. Next, blow into the jug several times. Now place the mouth of the jug against the lips, blow hard, and release the pressure suddenly. What happens? What happens if the jug is blown into again?

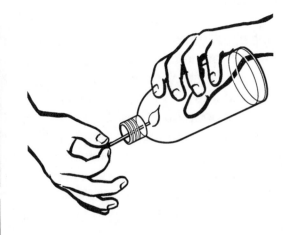

Materials Needed:

Match   Glass Jug

43

How Can We Make a Cloud?

Experiment/Demonstration #70

Procedure:

Fill a milk or juice bottle with hot water. Pour out most of the water, leaving about an inch in the bottom. Place an ice cube over the mouth of the bottle. Repeat the process using cold water. What happens in the two glass bottles?

Materials Needed:

Two Glass Bottles
Hot Water
Cold Water
Two Ice Cubes

How Can We Demonstrate Cloud Forms?

Experiment/Demonstration #71

Procedure:

Make daily observations of cloud types. If a member of the class has a camera with a good filter, such cloud photographs can be developed into an excellent exhibit.

Collect photographs of cloud types and arrange them as a bulletin board exhibit at the same relative levels as they occur in the atmosphere. Point out that observation of cloud movements is a valuable source of information to determine air movements at high altitude.

44

How Can We Demonstrate Dew?

Experiment/Demonstration #72

Procedure:

   Put some ice and water in a tin can or glass. Notice the drops of water on the outside of the can or glass. Dew is formed by some of the water vapor in the air changing to drops of water by cooling, such as on the tin can or glass.

Materials Needed:

Ice Water
Tin Can or Glass

How Can We Make Frost?

Experiment/Demonstration #73

Procedure:

   Place a wet piece of paper towel or cloth in a large covered beaker to raise the humidity. Then set a can containing a mixture of crushed ice and salt in the jar. Cover the jar again. A thick layer of frost should form. Compare the conditions within the jar with those under which natural frost forms.

Materials Needed:

Wet Paper Towel or Cloth
Large, Deep Beaker
Cover for Beaker
Can   Crushed Ice   Salt

What Is Sleet?

Experiment/Demonstration #74

Procedure:

Sleet is, simply stated, tiny frozen rain drops. To demonstrate this, fill a small test tube with water. Record the water temperature. Place the test tube with the thermometer in it into a jar of cracked ice (cubes) and salt. What happens to the water in the tube?

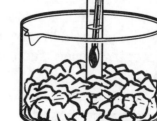

Materials Needed:

Small Test Tube   Jar
Thermometer   Salt
Crushed Ice   Water

What Is the Cause of Unequal Heating of the Land?

Experiment/Demonstration #75

Procedure:

Place some soil in one beaker and fill the other beaker with water to the same level. Allow the containers to remain in a shaded place until their temperatures are the same. Then set the beakers in direct sunlight. Support a thermometer in each beaker with the bulb just covered as shown in the diagram. Record the thermometer readings every 10 minutes. Which beaker gains heat faster?

Water

Soil

Materials Needed:

Soil   Water
Two Beakers   Support (ring stand)
Two Thermometers

Experiment/Demonstration #76

Procedure:

Show how the absorption of radiation varies with the color and nature of the surface on which solar energy falls. Obtain three similar tin cans and paint one black. Paint another white, and leave the third unpainted. Put an equal amount of water and a thermometer in each can. Set the cans at equal distances from an electric heater. Prepare a table for data and record the temperature of the water in each can at five-minute intervals. What happens to the water in each can?

Materials Needed:

Three Similar Cans   Water
Three Thermometers   Electric Heater
Black Paint

Experiment/Demonstration #77

Procedure:

Pour equal amounts of water into two test tubes, one of which is covered with black marker. Insert thermometers in each and set the two test tubes side by side in direct sunlight. What happens?

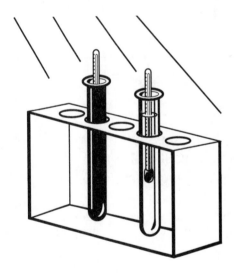

Materials Needed:

Two Test Tubes   Black Marker
Two Thermometers   Water
Beaker (to hold test tubes)

How Are Electric Charges Built up Before a Thunderstorm?

Experiment/Demonstration #78

Procedure:

Make a simple electrophorus to show how electric charges, such as those built up in clouds before thunderstorms, may be produced by induction. Cut a piece of inner tube about six inches square and tack it to a wooden block. Obtain a small pie tin and a stick of sealing wax. Melt one end of the stick of wax and force it against the inside of the pie tin to make an insulated handle as in the diagram. Briskly rub the piece of rubber with wool or fur to give it a charge. Set the pie tin on the charged rubber, touch the inside of the tin for an instant, and then pick up the plate by means of the insulated handle. The pie tin now has a charge.

Bring the pie tin near a pith ball to show that the tin has a charge. Now hold it near a metal faucet or radiator. The spark that jumps across the gap usually looks like a miniature flash of lightning and, like thunder, it can be heard.

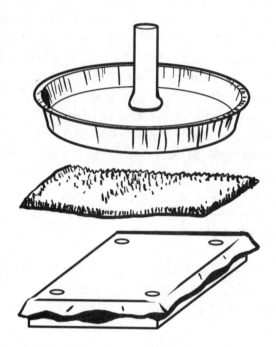

Materials Needed:

Small Pie Tin
Inner Tube (sheet of rubber)
Scissors (to cut rubber)
Stick of Sealing Wax
Wool or Fur
Wooden block
Tacks
Pith Ball

THE EARTH'S SURFACE

Through the use of experiments and demonstrations in this section, students can gain valuable insight into the composition and formation of the earth's surface. Hands-on experience with rocks, water, plants, minerals, and fossils will help students understand how rocks and the physical features of the earth's surface are broken down, changed, and formed.

Questions explored in this section include:

- How can we collect and study rocks?
- How can rock collections be made?
- What is the test for limestone?
- What do crystals look like?
- What is the difference between a rock and a mineral?
- What are the effects of water on rocks?
- How are new rocks formed?
- How are fossils formed?
- What effect do plants have on rocks?
- How does heating and cooling affect rocks?
- How does water wear away the earth's surface in some places and build it up in other places?
- How can we demonstrate the formation of stalactites and stalagmites in caves?
- How can we demonstrate some of the geological features formed by a stream?
- How can we demonstrate the action of ice in changing the earth's surface?
- How do we know that ice contains particles?
- Was this area covered by glaciers?
- How are kettle holes formed?
- Does air carry sediments?
- What does wind do to the debris on the ground?
- How are sand dunes formed?
- What are the forces that help make soil?
- What are the layers of the soil?
- What are the constituencies of soil?
- How is soil tested?
- How can we demonstrate soil erosion and conservation?
- How can models of the earth's surface be made from modeling clay, plaster of Paris, and papier mâché?
- How can a scale model be made?
- How is the earth's surface built up?
- How can we show a cause for faulting?
- How can a glass-sided trough be made?

How Can We Collect and Study Rocks?

Experiment/Demonstration #79

Procedure:

Ask each student to bring in one rock. A satisfactory sampling of local rocks can usually be obtained. Placing similar specimens together, divide the collected rocks into groups according to differences in shape, color, and other characteristics. Try to discover several different ways in which the rocks that have been collected may be grouped.

Select a single rock and try to learn as much about it as possible by careful observation alone. If a rock is flat, it is probably a piece of a layer of sediment that was laid down in water long ago and has since hardened. If it appears to be made up of sand grains cemented together, it is probably sandstone. If the rock is rounded, the wearing off of sharp corners is very likely the result of stream action. Granitelike rocks that have crystals of different colors were pushed up from deep in the earth long ago and cooled slowly. Rocks that differ greatly from most of the rocks found in the community were probably carried in by a glacier.

Careful observation of rock specimens using the developmental technique will serve to interest students in the further study of rocks. Many beginners will be curious to know the names of different rocks, but the identification of rocks will be of far less value than the development of their stories through careful observation of their characteristics. Identification, except for the most common kinds, might be avoided with beginners, since even experts cannot be sure of the name of a rock without testing it in a laboratory.

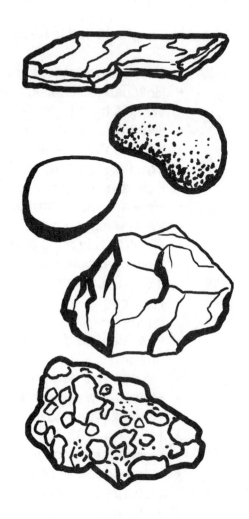

How Can Rock Collections Be Made?

Experiment/Demonstration #80

Procedure:

Encourage students to start small rock collections of their own. A good rock collection box can be purchased at a discount store or made from a cardboard box with a lid. If you are making your own box, use a nail and hammer to punch evenly-spaced holes in the box a short distance from the bottom. Run strings through the holes and around the bottom of the box and tie them tightly on the outside. The strings will then hold the specimens in position.

Cut small squares of adhesive tape and paste one square on each of the specimens collected. Number each specimen. Next make a key with a space for the name of each rock. Write in the names of any rocks that are known and paste the key on the cover of the box. Blank spaces can be filled in later if and when the names of the rocks are learned.

For beginners, it is best to keep the collections small and to confine them largely to local rocks. Students who have a special interest might want to learn how to use more elaborate techniques.

Materials Needed:

Box	String	Nail
Hammer	Rocks	Adhesive Tape

Experiment/Demonstration #81

Procedure:

Egg cartons are also convenient for small rock collections. Keys showing the position of each rock can be pasted on the inside or outside cover.

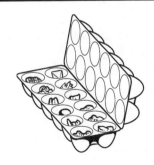

What Is the Test for Limestone?

Experiment/Demonstration #82

Procedure:

Some rock specimens collected will very likely resemble limestone. The test for limestone is to drop lemon juice on the surface of several specimens. Those that effervesce or bubble are limestone, and the gas given off is carbon dioxide. Scientists who study rocks use another acid called hydrochloric acid for this test, but lemon juice works almost as well and is much safer.

Lemon Juice

What Do Crystals Look Like?

Experiment/Demonstration #83

Procedure:

Examine a small quantity of sand and freshly broken rocks under a low-power microscope or a good hand lens. The almost-colorless crystals of sand are those of the mineral quartz, the most common mineral on Earth. Crystals of other minerals can also usually be found in sand. Crystals of different minerals will differ in size, shape, and color.

What Is the Difference Between a Rock and a Mineral?

Experiment/Demonstration #84

Procedure:

A rock is mineral matter found in the earth in large quantities. Most rocks are made up of mixtures of minerals, though some consist of only one mineral. A mineral is a chemical substance found in the earth but not formed by a plant or animal.

What Are the Effects of Water on Rocks?

Experiment/Demonstration #85

Procedure:

Place some small freshly-broken pieces of rock in a jar half-filled with clear water. Close the lid of the jar and shake the jar 100 times. What happens to the water in the jar? What happens after the jar has been shaken 1,000 times?

Materials Needed:

Jar With Lid
Freshly Broken Rocks
Clear Water

Experiment/Demonstration #86

Procedure:

Find some bricks or part of a curb that shows evidence of weathering. Collect pebbles from a stream that runs over a gravel or rock bed. Note their shape and texture. Rub pieces of different rocks together and note that all rocks are not of the same hardness.

How Are New Rocks Formed?

Experiment/Demonstration #87

Procedure:

What happens to the rock particles when rocks are broken and worn away? Observe the work done by running water on and near the school grounds when it rains. Call attention to the mud and small rocks that are carried away by streams, especially where the soil is not protected by a cover of vegetation.

The importance of soil conservation should be developed at this point. Find examples of destructive erosion near the school and discuss means of preventing erosion.

Since mud remains in running water as long as it keeps moving, a great deal of rock material finds its way into lakes or oceans. When the muddy water loses its forward motion, the rock particles settle to the bottom. The larger particles settle first, followed by the smaller. During times of flooding, which usually occur about once a year, enough material settles in the still water to make a layer. Each year a new layer of this sediment is deposited. As time goes on, the particles become pressed and cemented together and finally change into layers of rock.

About four-fifths of the land surface of the earth is covered with layers of rock that were laid down in water. These rocks are called sedimentary rocks. Changes in the levels of the oceans and continents have pushed many of these rocks upward where we see them today.

Experiment/Demonstration #88

Procedure:

On an outline map of the United States locate the mouths of the larger rivers. Indicate the regions offshore where sedimentary rocks are probably forming today.

Experiment/Demonstration #89

Procedure:

Sediments settle in water to form layers. Stir up a little coarse sand or gravel with some finer sand and soil, add water, and pour the mixture into a wide-mouth jar. Notice that the coarser particles settle to the bottom first, followed by the finer particles. When the water above the sediment becomes clear, siphon most of it off and add another layer in the same way. Additional layers may be added until the jar is nearly filled. The layer structure may then be clearly observed through the glass.

Call attention to the fact that lakes and ponds are rapidly disappearing all over the country as they become filled with sediment. Removal of vegetative cover hastens this process. How could we save our lakes and ponds?

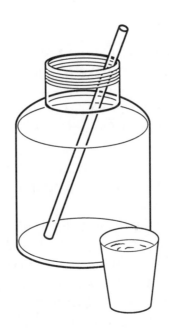

Materials Needed:

Large Wide-mouth Jar
Coarse Sand or Gravel
Fine Sand
Soil
Water
Tube for Siphoning

Use the following table as a basis for a discussion of how some common sedimentary rocks are formed:

Sediment	Process	Sedimentary Rock
Gravel	Cemented	Conglomerate
Shells	Cemented	Limestone
Sand	Cemented and Pressed	Sandstone
Clay or mud	Cemented and Pressed	Shale
Twigs and Leaves	Pressed	Coal

How Are Fossils Formed?

Experiment/Demonstration #90

Procedure:

Demonstrate the making of a plaster of Paris cast. First, make a rough estimate of the amount of plaster of Paris mixture desired and pour one-third of this amount of water in a cup, jar, or can. Sprinkle plaster of Paris into the water *without stirring* until small "islands" appear above the surface. This method will give the right proportion of plaster of Paris and water.

Now stir the mixture gently with a stick or spoon until it is smooth. It should have the consistency of melted ice cream or pancake batter. Pour the mixture into a greased mold or paper inserts used for muffins. The mixture will soon harden because the plaster of Paris unites chemically with the water.

If paper baking cups have been used, they can easily be removed from the casts because they are coated with paraffin wax. Such casts may be painted and decorated as desired and make attractive paper weights.

Plaster of Paris

Baking Cup

Materials Needed:

Plaster of Paris
Water
Mold or Paper Baking Cups
(Optional) Paints and Decorations

Experiment/Demonstration #91

Procedure:

Cover a leaf with petroleum jelly and lay it on a plane of glass. Around the leaf, place a circular strip of paper, plastic, or thin cardboard and press modeling clay against this collar to hold it in position. Now pour about one-half inch of plaster of Paris batter over the leaf. In about 15 minutes the paper and leaf can be removed and an excellent leaf print will result. This illustrates well the process of the formation of one type of fossil. Look for leaf prints in soft coal. Imprints of fern leaves are commonly found.

Plaster of Paris

Leaf Covered With Petroleum Jelly

Glass or Board

Leaf Imprint

Materials Needed:

Glass or Smooth Board   Plaster of Paris
Leaf (covered with petroleum jelly)
Water   Clay
Paper, Plastic, or Thin Cardboard

Experiment/Demonstration #92

Procedure:

Cover a shell such as a clam shell with petroleum jelly and pour wet plaster of Paris on it as was done in making a leaf print.

Experiment/Demonstration #93

Procedure:

Look through the classroom rock collection for evidence of fossils. Try to find additional fossil-bearing specimens to add to the plaster of Paris collection.

What Effect Do Plants Have on Rocks?

Experiment/Demonstration #94

Procedure:

Make a one-inch thick slab of plaster of Paris either in a straight-sided baking pan coated with petroleum jelly or by pouring the plaster into a wooden frame resting on a pane of glass. After the plaster has hardened, remove it from the mold.

Lay sprouted pea or bean seeds on the smooth side of the plaster and cover them with wet paper towels. Keep the slab (and seeds) in a terrarium so that the toweling stays moist. After several days remove the seeds. What happened to the surface of the plaster? Why?

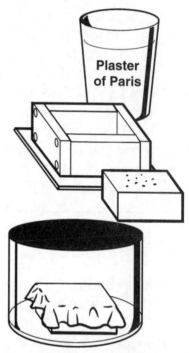

Plaster of Paris

Pea or Bean Sprouts Laying on the Plaster of Paris

Materials Needed:

Plaster of Paris
Pan or Wooden Frame
Sprouted Peas or Beans
Wet Paper Towels
Terrarium

Petroleum Jelly
Water

Experiment/Demonstration #95

Procedure:

Find rocks or rock ledges where mosses and lichens are growing. Scrape some of the plants off and notice that bits of rock flake off, loosened by the chemical action of the plants. A short field trip to see such a rock is an interesting learning activity.

How Does Heating and Cooling Affect Rocks?

Experiment/Demonstration #96

Procedure:

Completely fill a screw cap jar with water and tighten the cap. Wrap the jar completely in a piece of cloth or put it into a paper bag and allow it to freeze outdoors or in a house-hold freezer. What happens?

Materials Needed:

Screw Cap Jar (glass)   Water
Cloth or Paper Bag

Experiment/Demonstration #97

Procedure:

Carefully weigh a piece of dry porous rock such as sandstone or limestone. After soaking it in water overnight, reweigh the sample. What happened? What would happen if the rock were frozen?

Materials Needed:

Accurate Balance or Scales
Dry, Porous Rock   Water

Experiment/Demonstration #98

Procedure:

Wear goggles for this demonstration. Heat the end of a piece of glass tubing in a flame and plunge it quickly into cold water. Many rocks fracture in a similar way with heating and rapid cooling. Avoid heating samples of rock because there is a danger of explosion resulting from the conversion of absorbed water into steam.

How Does Water Wear Away the Earth's Surface in Some Places and Build It Up in Other Places?

Experiment/Demonstration #99

Procedure:

Make small drainage holes in the bottoms of several cans or flower pots and fill them with loose soil. Press down the soil so that it is even with the edges of the can. Place coins or flat stones on the surface of the soil, as shown in the diagram. Set each can in a large pan and sprinkle it with water. Continue the simulated rain until a change can be noted in the surface of the soil. Repeat this procedure, but set the pans of soil outdoors during a rain. What happens to the soil?

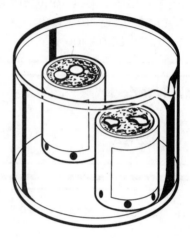

Materials Needed:

Cans or Flower Pots	"Rain"
Coins or Flat Stones	Large Pan
Soil	

Experiment/Demonstration #100

Procedure:

To demonstrate the impact of a raindrop, set a jar lid or saucer of soil in the center of a large sheet of paper. With a medicine dropper, release a few drops of water from a height of several feet on the soil and note the amount of soil that is splashed out on the paper. Place an obstacle such as a pencil in the path of the falling drops. This is comparable to a plant breaking the force of the water.

Materials Needed:

Jar Lid or Saucer	Pencil	Soil
Large Sheet of Paper	Medicine Dropper	

60

Experiment/Demonstration #101

Procedure:

Fill a flower pot with sandy soil or loam. Set the pot of soil in a basin under a dripping faucet for an hour or more. Notice how the clay and inorganic matter is removed from the surface by the falling drops.

Materials Needed:

Flower Pot   Sandy Soil or Loam
Dripping Faucet

Experiment/Demonstration #102

Procedure:

Build up a pile of sand and clay in a tray or other large vessel. Sprinkle it gently with a watering can. Note the erosion, the transportation of rock particles, and deposits made by the little streams that form.

Materials Needed:

Sand and Clay   Large Tray   Watering Can

Experiment/Demonstration #103

Procedure:

After a rain, explore school grounds for evidence of raindrop erosion. Look for splash erosion on the sides of the school building where pavement is next to the building, a grassy spot is near the building, and a bare soil spot is near the building. Notice if the building wall is equally clean in these different places.

Experiment/Demonstration #104

Procedure:

Punch holes in the bottoms of several metal pans, such as old baking tins. Cover the inside of the tins with paper towels and fill each with fine, dry soil. Just before a rain, set them out in different places on the school grounds where they will have different degrees of protection from the rain. After the rain, observe the soil in each tin. What happened to each and why?

Rain or splash sticks also show raindrop erosion. Paint some flat sticks or "laths" with white paint or tack pieces of white paper to them. Point one end of each stick so that it can be driven into the soil more easily. Before a rain, put out the rain sticks in various places around the school grounds, such as on bare ground, in grass, under a tree, near the building, or under the eaves.

After a rain, go out and observe the soil splashes on the sticks. Measure their distances from the ground. Tabulate this information and try to account for the differences in the height of the splashes.

Materials Needed:

Several Metal Pans
Paper Towels
Fine, Dry Soil
Flat Sticks or "Laths"
White Paint or White Paper

Experiment/Demonstration #105

Procedure:

After a heavy rain, collect jars of muddy water from a stream or from the gutter along the street. Let the water settle to see how much sediment it carried.

Experiment/Demonstration #106

Procedure:

Explore the school grounds for evidence of the transportation of soil by water. Sediment is often deposited along walks and driveways and in low places on the lawn.

Experiment/Demonstration #107

Procedure:

To show which materials in soil are carried away more readily, put some soil in a large jar half full of water. Shake the jar vigorously and then let the contents settle. What happens?

Materials Needed:

Soil
Large Jar (with lid)
Water

Experiment/Demonstration #108

Procedure:

Visit a stream and look for evidence of transportation of the soil by water, such as the muddiness of the stream, worn-away rocks, soil deposited in new places, and pieces of the bank broken off. Notice that the flat rocks in the bottom of streams are tilted in the direction opposite of the stream flow.

How Can We Demonstrate the Formation of Stalactites and Stalagmites in Caves?

Experiment/Demonstration #109

Procedure:

Study pictures of caves and possibly visit caves in the vicinity. Account for the formation of caves and sinkholes.

Closely related to cave formation is the formation of stalactites and stalagmites. The formation of miniature stalactites and stalagmites can be demonstrated by laying a cord between two small vessels filled with a saturated solution of Epsom salt as shown in the diagram. In caves, the material deposited is calcium carbonate, dissolved out by ground water.

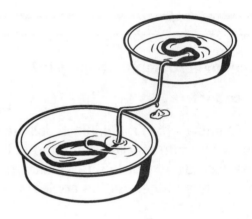

Materials Needed:

Cord   Water
Two Small Vessels   Epsom Salt

How Can We Demonstrate Some of the Geological Features Formed by a Stream?

Experiment/Demonstration #110

Procedure:

A very effective working model that shows erosion, transportation, and deposition of sediments can be set up easily. In a soil tray, place handfuls of soil, clay, sand, and gravel. Set the tray at a slight slope and run a rubber tube from the water tap to the closed end of the tray to provide a constantly flowing stream. By varying the rate of flow, the slope, and the materials in the tray, various geologic features can be produced in miniature.

How Can We Demonstrate the Action of Ice in Changing the Earth's Surface?

Experiment/Demonstration #111

Procedure:

Set a soil tray in a sloping position and fill it with soil. Put some ice or ice cubes at the top of the incline and notice what happens as they melt. Pick up one of the ice cubes and rub it over the soil. What happens?

Materials Needed:

Soil Tray   Soil   Ice

How Do We Know That Ice Contains Particles?

Experiment/Demonstration #112

Procedure:

Let an icicle melt on a piece of white paper or in a white pan. Notice that it has picked up small particles from the roof. The sediment from the icicle may be thought of as a miniature glacial deposit.

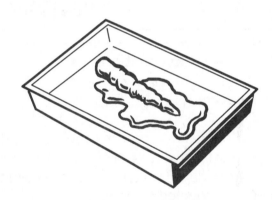

Was This Area Covered by Glaciers?

Experiment/Demonstration #113

Procedure:

Find out if the area in which you live was covered by glaciers. Locate evidence of glacial deposits, such as fields covered with stones and huge boulders in unusual places.

How Are Kettle Holes Formed?

Experiment/Demonstration #114

Procedure:

Kettle holes are depressions where drainage water collects. Since there is no outlet to carry the water away, kettle holes often help maintain a relatively high water table over a wide area. They are believed to have been formed in glacial times by the melting of large blocks of ice beneath the surface when a glacier receded. The formation of a kettle hole can be demonstrated by placing one or more ice cubes on a pan and covering them with soil so that the surface is level. When the ice cubes melt, an excellent model of a kettle hole is formed.

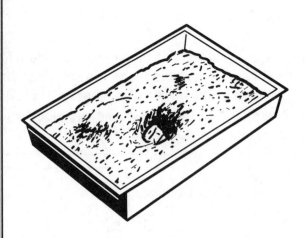

Does Air Carry Sediments?

Experiment/Demonstration #115

Procedure:

To show that air carries sediment, set a white pan filled with water out on the windowsill. After a day or two, observe the sediment that has collected in the pan.

What Does Wind Do to the Debris on the Ground?

Experiment/Demonstration #116

Procedure:

On a windy day, observe what the wind does to leaves, twigs, and other debris on the ground. Look in corners protected from the wind and notice that soil, leaves, and other materials are sometimes deposited there.

How Are Sand Dunes Formed?

Experiment/Demonstration #117

Procedure:

Pour a pile of dry sand or powdered soap on the bottom of a large carton cut away as shown in the diagram. Turn an electric fan on the pile and notice how the particles are moved. Notice that more particles are moved as the velocity of the wind increases. Put an obstacle such as a pencil or finger in the path of the blowing sand and relate this to snow fences and sand dunes.

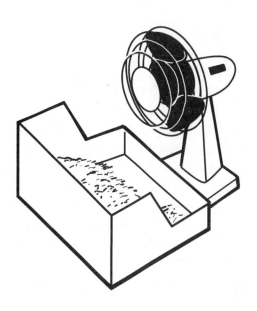

Materials Needed:

Dry Sand or Powdered Soap   Pencil
Large Carton (box)   Electric Fan

What Are the Forces That Help Make Soil?

Experiment/Demonstration #118

Procedure:

Place one of the larger flat pieces of rock from the classroom collection on a piece of newspaper and rub a smaller rock over it. Continue rubbing until some rock dust is worn from the rocks. Examine the dust and compare it to soil.

The activities of animals, the action of freezing and thawing, the force of gravity, the work of streams, and many other factors are continually rubbing rocks together and wearing them away. With the aid of plants, the dust that is worn from rocks may eventually become good soil.

Grass fires, forest fires, and wasteful farming practices remove the cover of vegetation and allow the soil to erode. It takes many years to form good soil, so conserving soil is very important.

What Are the Layers of Soil?

Experiment/Demonstration #119

Procedure:

Visit a steep hillside and measure the depth of topsoil at the top and bottom of the slope. Dig holes about the size of post-holes to find the dividing line between topsoil and subsoil. Be sure to replace the soil that is removed.

What Are the Constituencies of Soil?

Experiment/Demonstration #120

Procedure:

Put a handful of soil into a tall glass jar or bottle with water and stir the soil and water thoroughly. Shake the bottle or jar vigorously until both soil and water are thoroughly mixed. Put the jar or bottle where it will not be disturbed. The next day three layers or kinds of materials will be visible:

a. on the bottom: sand—the heaviest material, consisting of tiny bits of rocks.
b. second layer: clay or ground up rock particles.
c. top layer: decayed plant and animal material.

Materials Needed:

Soil   Water
Large Glass Jar or Bottle (With Lid)

How Is Soil Tested?

Experiment/Demonstration #121

Procedure:

Carry on a soil-testing experiment, using a regular soil-testing kit if one is available. Follow the directions included with the kit and discuss the importance of maintaining correct soil conditions for various crops. Point out reasons why some soils become too acidic and explain why lime is used to neutralize the acid. If a regular soil-testing kit is not available, satisfactory results can be obtained by adding a sample of soil to some water in a beaker. Allow the mixture to settle until there is a layer of clear water at the top. This water will contain dissolved matter and can be tested with litmus or pH paper.

Experiment/Demonstration #122

Procedure:

To test soil, obtain several soil samples from different areas. Place some soil from each sample in paper cups and label them, denoting areas from which each came. Add enough water to make the soil fairly moist. Place a piece of each type of litmus paper in each cup (blue and red). After five minutes, remove the litmus papers from each cup and place them in front of their respective cups. What types of soil have been tested? If the blue litmus paper turns red, the soil is acidic in nature. If the red litmus paper turns blue, the soil is base or alkali in nature. If neither type of paper changes color, the soil is not an acid or a base.

Materials Needed:

Soil Samples   Litmus Paper
Cups   Water

How Can We Demonstrate Soil Erosion and Conservation?

Experiment/Demonstration #123

Procedure:

A pair of wooden, or plastic, troughs or trays similar to those in the diagram represent a very effective device for conducting various soil conservation and erosion experiments. Such troughs can be made quickly in the woodshop or even in the classroom. For best results, the troughs should be not less than two feet in length and six inches in width, closed at one end. A little caulking around the inside corners will make them watertight (which is not necessary if plastic trays are used.)

Pieces of wire mesh or screen should be tacked over the open ends of the troughs as shown. Large funnels and plastic bottles and ordinary buckets can be used to catch the overflow water.

On practically every school campus a suitable place can be found for carrying out conservation experiments and demonstrations outdoors. The following experiments can, however, be conducted indoors as well as outdoors.

a. Fill one tray with loose soil and the other with firmly-packed soil. With both trays tilted slightly, water each equally with a garden sprinkler or a large coffee can with holes punched in the bottom. Which tray loses more soil?

b. Fill both trays with soil, but cover one with sod. Water both trays equally. Which tray loses more soil?

c. Fill both trays with soil, but give one more slope than the other. Water both trays equally. Which tray loses more soil?

Possibilities for additional experiments are obvious and are often suggested by students.

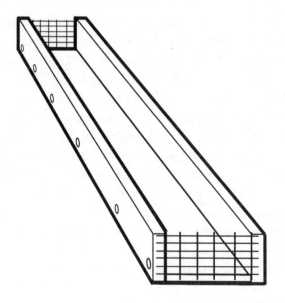

Materials Needed:

Two Wood or Plastic Trays (not less than two feet by six inches and closed at one end)

Wire Screen   Tacks
Funnels/Bottles/Buckets
Soil   Sod
Sprinkler

How Can a Model of the Earth's Surface Be Made From Modeling Clay?

Experiment/Demonstration #124

Procedure:

Temporary idealized models can be made from modeling clay. If the model is to be rather large, make an armature of pieces of wood and wire screening that follow the approximate outlines of the finished model; or make a wire armature and stuff it with crumpled newspaper to resemble the shape of the finished model. Clay can then be pressed into the foundation and worked into the desired shape. Keep damp cloth over the model until it is finished to prevent the clay from drying out too rapidly.

How Can a Model of the Earth's Surface Be Made From Plaster of Paris?

Experiment/Demonstration #125

Procedure:

A plaster of Paris model may be cast from a clay model. Build a wooden frame around the clay model, making its depth greater than that of the model. Pour plaster of Paris into the form. It is better to prepare too much plaster than too little as it sets quickly and will crack if a second mixture is added. Let the plaster harden for a day or so and then carefully remove the clay model. This will produce a plaster of Paris mold that shows the model in reverse. Coat the mold with a layer of petroleum jelly. Now prepare a new mixture of plaster of Paris and pour it into the mold. After a day or so, separate the mold from the new model. The surface of the model may be smoothed by rubbing with sandpaper and then painted if desired.

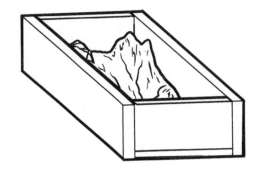

71

How Can a Model of the Earth's Surface Be Made From Papier Mâché?

Experiment/Demonstration #126

Procedure:

Lighter models may be made with papier mâché. First, prepare a clay model as previously described. Soak strips of newspaper in a bucket of water for several days and add some starch paste. Place strips of the soaked newspaper over the model in an even layer about one-fourth inch thick. Let the paper dry thoroughly, then remove the clay model. After the model is dry, give it a sizing coat of glue or shellac and paint it as desired.

Another method is to make a wire armature in the general shape of the feature desired. Then coat one-inch strips of dry newspaper with library paste and build them up over the armature to a thickness of about one-fourth inch. Let it dry thoroughly.

How Can a Scale Model Be Made?

Experiment/Demonstration #127

Procedure:

Scale models are not difficult to make. From a topographic map of the area to be reproduced, enlarge each contour on a separate sheet of thick cardboard or wallboard. Enlargement of the topographic map can be done by using transparencies and overhead projectors to trace the shapes. Cut out each contour separately. Then stack them together and paste or tack in proper position. The result is a relief map of the region, to scale.

Relief maps with smoother surfaces can be made by smoothing the surface of the cardboard with modeling clay or plaster of Paris. The map can then be painted in appropriate colors.

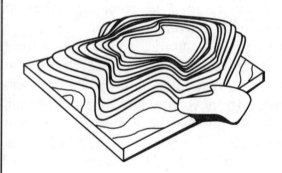

How Is the Earth's Surface Built Up?

Experiment/Demonstration #128

Procedure:

To show what happens to horizontal stratums of sedimentary rock when they are compressed laterally, stack several thin sheets of colored plasticene on each other. Then place a hand near each end of the stack and push toward the middle. The stacked materials form a hump or mountain. Slice the ridges crosswise with a knife to show the curved rock layers (synclines and anticlines).

Layers of plasticene after pressure has been applied.

Materials Needed:

Several Thin Sheets of Colored Plasticene
Knife

How Can We Show a Cause for Faulting?

Experiment/Demonstration #129

Procedure:

To show how accumulated sediments may cause faulting, balance two books close together on the two arms of a platform balance. The pages of the books will represent the rock layers. On one book set a pan of sand to represent a mountain. On the other, set a pan of water to represent an ocean. Point out that as the mountain erodes, sediments are carried into the ocean. Represent this by taking a teaspoonful of sand from the mountain and dumping it into the ocean. This disturbs the balance of the earth's crust and causes a fault (earthquake).

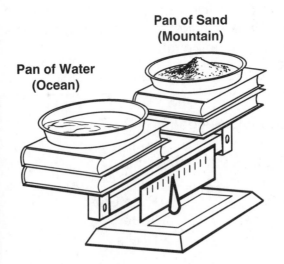

Pan of Sand
(Mountain)

Pan of Water
(Ocean)

The books represent rock layers

Materials Needed:

Two Books (same size)   Pan of Water
Platform Balance   Pan of Sand
Teaspoon

How Can a Glass-Sided Trough be Made?

Experiment/Demonstration #130

Procedure:

A glass-sided trough as shown in the diagram is a simple project for a metal shop and makes possible several interesting experiments. The frame of the trough is cut from 20-gauge or heavier galvanized iron. The corners are soldered together and braced with triangular pieces of the same metal. The outlets are short pieces of metal tubing soldered into holes cut into one end of the frame.

The frame is fastened to a base of three-fourths-inch plywood by nails that are later covered with solder to prevent leakage. The sides are double thickness window glass or plate glass, held in place with modeling clay or plasticene, which makes a tight joint and yet allows easy removal.

The trough can be filled with different combinations and arrangements of rock and soil material. The water level can be controlled by placing small corks in the ends of the tubes. A model artesian well can also be formed in the trough.

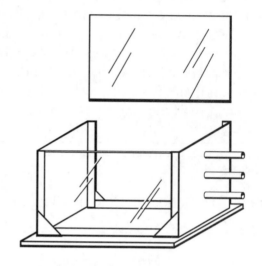

Materials Needed:

20-gauge Galvanized Iron
Metal Tubing $\frac{3}{4}$-inch Plywood
Nails   Plate Glass
Plasticene   Water
Corks   Rocks
Soil

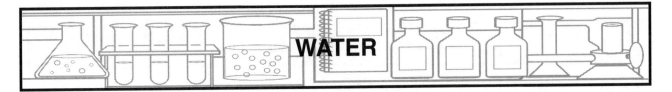

WATER

Where water resources are not used wisely, other natural resources, such as soil, forests, and wildlife, also begin to disappear. Through the learning activities suggested in this section, students should gain understanding and appreciation of the sources of water, how a safe water supply is provided, and how it can be conserved.

Questions explored in this section include:

- Does water exert pressure?
- What is the water table?
- What is the effect of lowering the water table?
- Upon what does the height of the water table depend?
- What is the evidence that the water table is near the surface?
- How can the amount of runoff water be reduced?
- What is the effect of the water table on seedlings?
- How can we chemically remove impurities from water?
- How can we filter water?
- How can we distill water?
- What is the function of soap?
- What is the disadvantage of hard water?
- How can we make water softer?
- How can we make water "wetter"?

Does Water Exert Pressure?

Experiment/Demonstration #131

Procedure:

Fasten a piece of sheet rubber over a thistle tube and attach the tube to a manometer. The rubber can be cut from a balloon. Hold the end of the thistle tube at various depths under water. What happens?

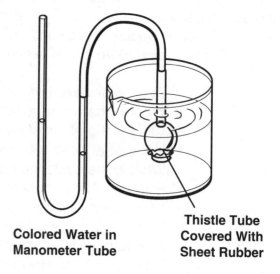

Colored Water in Manometer Tube

Thistle Tube Covered With Sheet Rubber

Materials Needed:

Rubber (From a Balloon)   Water
Ruler   Thistle Tube
Water   Large Beaker
Manometer

Experiment/Demonstration #132

Procedure:

The difference in water pressure on different floors in some buildings is very noticeable. The milk carton demonstration shown in the diagram should provide a basis for understanding the reason. Adjust the supply entering the carton so that the water continues to flow from all four holes in the side of the carton.

Some students may not know that very tall buildings have water supply tanks above the top floor. A picture showing the rooftops of any older city will reveal many of these tanks. In more modern buildings these tanks are enclosed by the roof or placed in a tower.

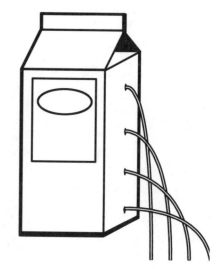

Materials Needed:

Milk Carton   Flowing Water

What Is the Water Table?

Experiment/Demonstration #133

Procedure:

A simple model that can be set up within a few seconds presents an excellent approach to the concept of the water table. Hold a large-bore glass tube against the side of a large deep beaker to represent a well. Fill the beaker with sand, and pour water on the sand until the water level rises about halfway. Note that the water level is the same outside the well (glass tube) as it is inside the well. Paste a narrow strip of wet paper on the beaker to mark the water level and discuss the term *water table*.

Use a demonstration lift pump to remove some of the water from the well and call attention to the lowering of the water table.

Water
Table

What Is the Effect of Lowering the Water Table?

Experiment/Demonstration #134

Procedure:

The effect of lowering the water table can be effectively illustrated by using a demonstration pump and an aquarium filled with sand and water as shown in the diagram. The well and the pond go dry as water is pumped from the glass tube into the beaker. An empty plastic toothpaste tube pressed against the side of the aquarium can be used as the well casing in place of a glass tube.

When the well and the pond have been drained, the water table can be raised again by reversing the position of the pump. A short piece of rubber tubing can be attached to the spout of the pump so that water can be pumped from the beaker back into the well.

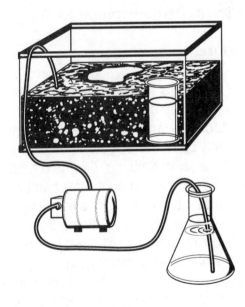

Upon What Does the Height of the Water Table Depend?

Experiment/Demonstration #135

Procedure:

The source of water in the soil is rainfall. The height of the water table therefore mainly depends upon how well water penetrates the soil. A large amount of runoff occurs when soils are relatively impervious to water. Most of this runoff water is carried away by streams and does not help raise the water table. To determine the permeability of soil, a metal can should be opened at both ends with a rotary can opener so that the rims are smooth. Press the can into the ground to a distance of about one inch and fill it completely with water. Use a watch to determine the time required for all the water to go into the soil. Repeat the procedure in different places so the data can be summarized into a table.

What Is the Evidence That the Water Table Is Near the Surface?

Experiment/Demonstration #136

Procedure:

Ask students to mention places where there is evidence that the water table is near the surface. Swampy or marshy locations can usually be found at a distance that is not too far for a short field trip. During a field trip of this kind, one significant observation that can be made is the difference in the vegetation in wet and dry areas. If the field trip is taken in early spring, it will often be possible to find the water table by digging a small hole with a shovel. Attention should be called to the fact that the water table is usually nearer the surface in spring than at other times of the year.

How Can the Amount of Runoff Water be Reduced?

Experiment/Demonstration #137

Procedure:

The importance of reducing the amount of runoff water can be shown by comparing an area protected by vegetation and one that is not so protected. The protected area will be more moist. Water from previous rains will still be helping to maintain the water table in the protected area. The unprotected area will be depleting the water table. Suitable areas for comparison can often be located on or near the school campus or in a nearby park. The effects of unwise farming practices, the building of dams and reservoirs, and the construction of drainage ditches can also be related to the water table. The question of whether or not the local community has a water table problem and what might be done about it should also be considered.

What Is the Effect of the Water Table on Seedlings?

Experiment/Demonstration #138

Procedure:

The effect of the height of the water table on the germination and growth of seedlings can easily be demonstrated as shown in the diagram. Observe the growth of the seedlings and also observe capillary action in soil. It shows in addition that the water table must be constantly replenished because of water lost by evaporation at the surface.

Low
Water Table

High
Water Table

Materials Needed:

Two Graduated Cylinders   Soil
Two Thistle Tubes   Beans
Water

How Can We Chemically Remove Impurities From Water?

Experiment/Demonstration #139

Procedure:

Put some muddy water in a tall jar and add a small amount of alum crystals. Stir the mixture and allow it to settle. The alum forms a jellylike mass that entangles the dirt particles and carries them down as it settles. This process, which is called coagulation, is used by many cities in removing suspended matter from the water supply.

Materials Needed:

Muddy Water   Jar
Alum Crystals

Experiment/Demonstration #140

Procedure:

Pour off some water obtained from the coagulation demonstration in #139. Heat a sample in a beaker over a burner to evaporate the water. Turn off the burner just as the final water boils away. Allow the beaker to cool and examine the contents. The deposit in the beaker is similar to that which forms inside a teakettle and in boiler pipes. Emphasize that filtering and coagulation do not remove mineral matter.

Materials Needed:

Water   Beaker
Burner

Experiment/Demonstration #141

Procedure:

Chlorine is added to most city water to destroy bacteria. Set a large vessel in a sink and quickly half-fill it with cold water. If chlorine is present it will be possible to smell, sniffing close to the top of the vessel. Allow chlorinated water to stand for half an hour and smell it again. Practically all the chlorine will have escaped.

Experiment/Demonstration #142

Procedure:

It is of course dangerous to drink water from sources that are not known to be safe. In emergencies, water from lakes and streams can be made safe to drink. Water purifying tablets may be obtained from outdoor camping supply houses.

How Can We Filter Water?

Experiment/Demonstration #143

Procedure:

Support a large glass funnel on a ring stand. Fill the funnel with clean pebbles, coarse sand and fine sand, as shown in the diagram. Pour some muddy water through this filter unit. Call attention to the fact that although most of the solid impurities have been removed, the water is still not safe for drinking.

Materials Needed:

Large Glass Funnel	Pebbles
Coarse/Fine Sand	Ring Stand
Muddy Water	Beaker

How Can We Distill Water?

Experiment/Demonstration #144

Procedure:

Arrange a simple distillation unit as shown in the diagram. Pour some of the impure water into the large beaker and heat until some water collects on the smaller beaker. This water will be practically free from impurities. Save the distilled water for subsequent demonstrations.

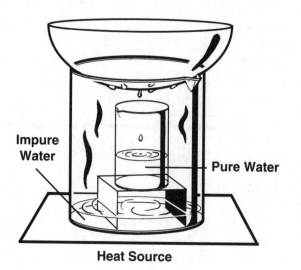

Impure Water

Pure Water

Heat Source

Materials Needed:

Tall 500 ml Beaker
Bent Metal Platform
50 ml Beaker
Evaporating Dish (or Watch Glass)
Impure Water

What Is the Function of Soap?

Experiment/Demonstration #145

Procedure:

Add a few drops of cooking oil to half a test tube of water and shake the tube vigorously. Notice that the oil is broken up into drops that soon come together again. Now add a little soap powder, shake the tube again, and notice the drops disappear. The oil is broken up into very fine droplets, forming an emulsion. These droplets can easily be rinsed away.

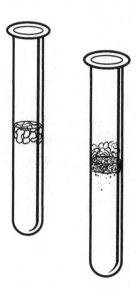

Materials Needed:

Test Tube   Cooking Oil
Water   Soap Powder

Experiment/Demonstration #146

Procedure:

Rub some grease on a piece of cloth and try to wash it out with water. Repeat with soapy water. Student's hands washed in ordinary water and then with soap are also sometimes an effective demonstration.

Materials Needed:

Cloth   Grease
Water   Soap

What Is the Disadvantage of Hard Water?

Experiment/Demonstration #147

Procedure:

Add a teaspoonful of Epsom salt to a large beaker half full of tap water to make some very hard water. In a similar beaker, half full of water, dissolve some soap chips. Now pour the contents of one beaker into the other and notice the scum that forms. Feel the scum and notice how sticky it is. In hard water, much soap is wasted because it combines with chemicals in the water and can no longer perform its cleansing action.

Materials Needed:

Soap Powder   Two Beakers
Epsom Salt   Water

How Can We Make Water Softer?

Experiment/Demonstration #148

Procedure:

Mix a little borax or other water softener in a small quantity of water. Make some hard water by adding a few Epsom salt crystals to about a pint of tap water. Now set four test tubes in a rack, each filled about three-quarters full as follows:

(1) Hard water plus 10 drops water softener
(2) Hard water with no softener
(3) Tap water plus 10 drops water softener
(4) Tap water without water softener

Add liquid soap to each test tube, drop by drop, shaking well after each drop until lasting suds are formed. Summarize the results in a table and interpret it.

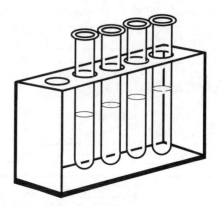

Materials Needed:

Washing Soda	Water
Borax	Four Test Tubes
Epsom Salt	Test Tube Rack
Soap	

How Can We Make Water "Wetter"?

Experiment/Demonstration #149

Procedure:

A simple demonstration of "making water wetter" can be shown to assist students in understanding the action of soaps and detergents. Fill two beakers with cold water and add two teaspoonfuls of a detergent to one and stir until dissolved. Sprinkle some pepper, aluminum powder, or talcum powder on the surface of the plain water and then on the surface of the water containing the detergent. What happens?

AIRPLANES, JETS, AND ROCKETS

In order to develop an understanding of how an airplane flies, it is important to begin with verbalizations of theories and principles. Through a wide variety of firsthand experiences, students can learn, for example, that the pressure of moving air decreases as its speed becomes greater. After students have gained a considerable background of experience, the need will arise for a few technical terms to describe the effects of the flow of air around objects. These terms will then be easy to learn because they will have some meaning.

Students are more fascinated than ever before with the possibilities of space travel and the problems of outer space. They want to know why satellites do not fall to the earth, how rocket ships and space platforms may be constructed, and whether life exists on other worlds. Because these problems involve learning about gravity, flight, life, air, light, and heat, the study of space furnishes an opportunity to develop important science concepts.

Access to Internet information should lend added interest to the study of airplanes, jets, and rockets. Effective use can also be made of plane models, model building kits, supplies obtainable at hobby shops and the facilities of nearby airports.

The following questions will be explored in this section:

- How does changing air pressure affect objects?
- How is a plane lifted?
- How is thrust provided by propellers?
- How is lift provided by an airplane?
- How can we demonstrate drag?
- How can we demonstrate thrust in jets and rockets?
- How can we demonstrate the principle of the helicopter?
- How can we demonstrate the function of the elevators and the rudders?
- How can we demonstrate the function of ailerons?
- What are seat belts used for?
- How can we make a parachute?
- What is meant by centrifugal force?

How Does Changing Air Pressure Affect Objects?

Experiment/Demonstration #150

Procedure:

Cut a short piece of drinking straw. The person with the straw should hold his or her head back so that the straw is vertical and then blow hard through the straw. Then place a ping-pong ball very carefully in the stream of air. It can be held several inches above the straw as long as the air supply lasts.

Materials Needed:

Drinking Straw   Ping-pong Ball

Experiment/Demonstration #151

Procedure:

Tie strings to two apples and suspend them from a support an inch or two apart. Ask students to blow between the apples and try to blow them further apart. Instead of moving farther apart, the apples bump together because the air moving between them reduces the air pressure.

Materials Needed:

Support   String
Two Apples   Straw

Experiment/Demonstration #152

Procedure:

Inflate a toy balloon and close the opening with string. Tilt an electric fan upward and place the balloon in the air stream. The balloon remains in the stream because the pressure of the surrounding air is greater than that in the stream. Attach one or more paper clips to the string and note that the balloon exerts a lifting force.

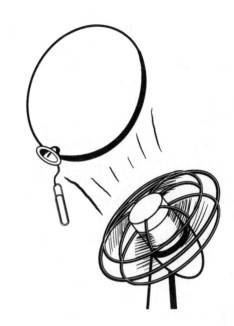

Materials Needed:

Balloon	String
Electric Fan	Paper Clips

Experiment/Demonstration #153

Procedure:

Bend down the edges of a card so that it is held about one-half inch above a table. With a drinking straw, blow air under the card. Explain what happens in terms of the relative pressures of still air and moving air.

Roll a card until it is permanently curved and set it upright on a table. With another card, brush air past the convex surface and note the direction the card falls.

Materials Needed:

Three Sheets of Thin Cardboard
Drinking Straw

How Is a Plane Lifted?

Experiment/Demonstration #154

Procedure:

Fasten a small model plane above one platform of a platform balance as shown in the diagram. Use modeling clay or some other convenient means of holding it in position and balance it carefully with weights. Direct air from an electric fan toward the wing. What happens?

Materials Needed:

Model Airplane   Support (for Plane)
Modeling Clay   Platform Balance
Electric Fan

How Is Thrust Provided by Propellers?

Experiment/Demonstration #155

Procedure:

The force that drives airplanes forward is known as thrust. In conventional airplanes, thrust is provided by the propeller. The effect of this force can be easily observed. On a smooth table, place a board on top of three round pencils, making sure the board will roll easily. Place a portable electric fan on top of the board. What happens?

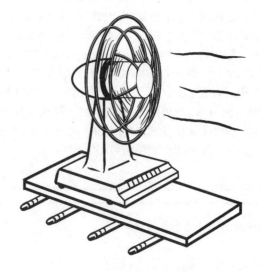

Materials Needed:

Smooth Board   Electric Fan
Three Round Pencils

How Is Lift Provided by an Airplane?

Experiment/Demonstration #156

Procedure:

Cut a strip of paper nine inches long and two inches wide. Hold it by the narrow end and blow across the upper surface of the paper. What happens to the paper?

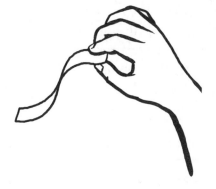

Materials Needed:

Scissors   Paper

How Can We Demonstrate Drag?

Experiment/Demonstration #157

Procedure:

To show drag, obtain a piece of cardboard about three inches square. Light a candle and place it vertically on a table or dish. Place the cardboard about two or three inches from the candle and secure it with a bit of clay or tape. Blow hard against the secured card. What happens to the flame?

Materials Needed:

Cardboard   Tape or Modeling Clay
Candle

Experiment/Demonstration #158

Procedure:

Obtain a piece of flexible cardboard about three inches by 10 inches. Bend the ends of the cardboard as shown and fasten them with glue and/or paper clips. Place the cardboard near the candle with the clipped ends nearest the candle. Blow against the curved end. What happens?

Materials Needed:

Flexible Cardboard   Candle
Glue/Paper Clips

How Can We Demonstrate Thrust in Jets and Rockets?

Experiment/Demonstration #159

Procedure:

Rockets and jet-propelled aircraft, as well as propeller-driven planes, move forward by means of thrust. The thrust of rockets and jets is caused by the flow of hot gases from the exhaust. Blow up a balloon and release it. The rapid escape of air pushes the balloon in the opposite direction. This illustrates the fundamental principle of jet propulsion.

Materials Needed:

Balloon

Experiment/Demonstration #160

Procedure:

Construct a toy jet balloon as shown in the illustration. Stretch a smooth wire or string across a room. Attach lengths of string to a long balloon so that it hangs parallel to the wire. Place paper clips on the wire and blow up the balloon. As it deflates, the balloon will be propelled along the wire. The speed of the balloon rocket may be modified by squeezing the opening of the tube. (The tube is made of a $1\frac{1}{2}$-inch square of paper, shaped around a pencil, taped, and inserted into the neck of the balloon.)

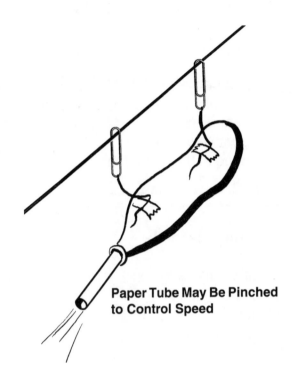

Paper Tube May Be Pinched to Control Speed

Materials Needed:

Smooth Wire $1\frac{1}{2}$ inch square of paper
Two Paper Clips   Tape
Long Balloon   String

Experiment/Demonstration #161

Procedure:

Build a simple jet engine. Punch a small hole near the edge of the bottom of a small can. Mount the can so that it will stand horizontally on wires with the hole at the top. Half fill the can with water and replace the cover. Mount the can on top of the plastic dish or container so that the candle flame will be directly under it. When the water boils, steam will issue forth from the pin hole jet. To do this, the steam must also push forward on the "boiler." Because of this push, the boat will speed across the pan of water.

Materials Needed:

Small Empty Can (with lid)   Wire
Small Plastic Container That Will Float
Pan of Water   Candle

Experiment/Demonstration #162

Procedure:

Suspend a small bottle by two threads. Place a tablespoonful of rubbing alcohol in the bottle and cork it. Carefully heat the bottle with a candle flame. What happens to the bottle as the cork pops out?

Materials Needed:

Small Bottle (with cork)   Stand
Rubbing Alcohol   Thread
Candle

Experiment/Demonstration #163

Procedure:

Lay a small bottle on two round pencils so that it rolls easily. Wrap a teaspoonful of baking soda in a small piece of paper and place it in the bottle. Place a tablespoonful of vinegar in the bottle and cork it loosely. What happens?

Materials Needed:

Small Bottle (with cork)   Baking Soda
Vinegar   Pencils (Round)
Paper

Experiment/Demonstration #164

Procedure:

Show that a jet of water, as well as a jet of air, can cause a thrust. Attach a piece of rubber tubing about a foot long to the end of a glass or metal funnel. Heat a piece of glass tubing about four inches long and bend it to form a right angle. Attach the bent glass tube to the lower end of the rubber tube. Hold the funnel upright and pour water into it. What happens?

Materials Needed:

Rubber Tubing   Funnel (glass or metal)
Glass Tubing   Water

Experiment/Demonstration #165

Procedure:

Punch several nail holes around a metal coffee can near the bottom. Push the nail sidewise in the same direction before removing it from each hole. Suspend the can as shown in the diagram and fill it with water. What happens?

Materials Needed:

Large Coffee Can   Water
Nail   Hammer
String

How Can We Demonstrate the Principle of the Helicopter?

Experiment/Demonstration #166

Procedure:

Cut out a piece of paper as shown in the diagram. Fold over the bottom section as shown and fasten it with a paper clip. Throw the device into the air and it will spin rapidly as it falls. The spin causes an upward thrust, but this is not sufficient to lift the helicopter. However, there is enough thrust to reduce the rate of fall. Helicopters can use this method of landing in the event of engine failure.

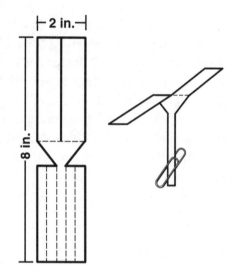

Materials Needed:

Paper   Scissors   Paper Clip

Experiment/Demonstration #167

Procedure:

Make the four cuts in a sheet of paper five inches square as shown. Bend the four corners toward the center and put a pin through the five holes indicated to form a pinwheel. The point of the pin is placed in the end of the eraser of an ordinary pencil. When this device is dropped from a window or stairwell, its fall is slowed down by the upward thrust of the revolving pinwheel. Many times, helicopters can land safely even when the motor stops.

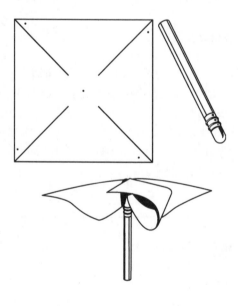

Materials Needed:

Paper   Scissors
Pin   Pencil

Experiment/Demonstration #168

Procedure:

From a strip of soft wood six inches long, one inch wide, and one-fourth inch thick, cut away the edges as shown in the diagram. Bore a small hole in the center and fit a dowel rod into it. Spin the dowel between the hands very rapidly and the device will rise into the air as a helicopter does. The rotating propeller blades push the air downward and the reaction or thrust forces the helicopter upward.

Some helicopters have a motor-driven propeller. In some, jet engines are mounted at the ends of the wings. These operate on a principle similar to that of the rotary lawn sprinkler.

Try spinning the helicopter model at a slight angle and it will travel in a sidewise direction. The movements of a real helicopter are controlled by varying the tilt and pitch of the rotating wings.

Materials Needed:

Soft Wood
Dowel Rod

How Can We Demonstrate the Function of the Elevators and Rudders?

Experiment/Demonstration #169

Procedure:

On a three by five-inch card or piece of cardboard cut from a notebook, paste a vertical cardboard fin as shown in the diagram. Leave the rear portion of the fin free by extending it beyond the card. Find the point where the card balances and push a thumbtack through it into the cork of a bottle. The card should now turn easily.

Blow through a drinking straw directing the air across the top of the card. Turn the card slightly and blow across it. It turns back and faces the wind, illustrating the function of the vertical fin of the airplane.

Bend the unattached portion of the fin to the left along the vertical dotted line shown in the diagram. Again blow air over the cardboard. Bend it to the right and repeat. Note the movement of the card. This illustrates the function of the rudder.

If the rudder is turned to the right, the wind forces the tail to the left while the nose moves to the right. The opposite effect is noted if the rudder is turned to the left.

Make the two cuts on the rear of the card. Bend the two portions of the trailing edge of the card upward to represent the elevators in raised position. Blow across the top of the card and note that the rear of the card goes down. Bend the elevators down and repeat.

Adjust both the elevators and the rudders in different ways to show they work together.

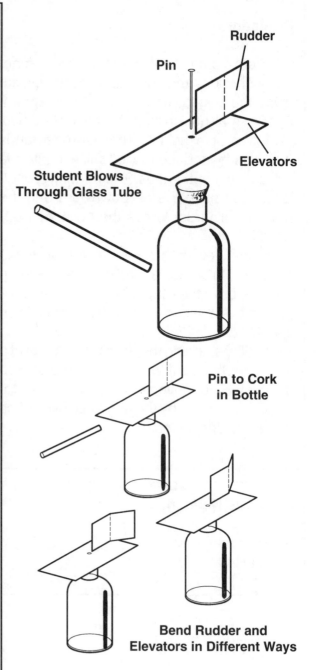

Rudder

Pin

Elevators

Student Blows
Through Glass Tube

Pin to Cork
in Bottle

Bend Rudder and
Elevators in Different Ways

Materials Needed:

Drinking Straw	Paste	Index Card
Cork	Bottle	Scissors
Cardboard	Thumbtack	

How Can We Demonstrate the Function of the Ailerons?

Experiment/Demonstration #170

Procedure:

Remove the cardboard from the back of an ordinary writing tablet. Cut a plane model similar to the diagram so that the wingspread and length from nose to tail are both about eight inches. Attach a string about a foot long to the nose of the plane. Allow the plane to hang straight down on the end of the string. Pull the string upward slowly. Note that the plane has little or no spin. Make the two cuts on the rear of the wings as shown. Bend one edge down and one up. Now pull the string upward slowly and note the direction of spin. Reverse the position of the bent parts and again note the direction of spin. This shows the function of the ailerons.

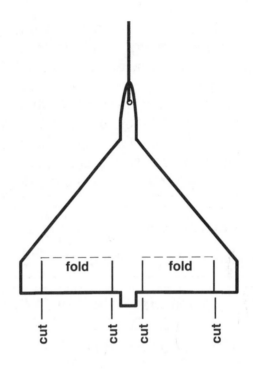

Materials Needed:

Cardboard   Scissors   Thread

Air Safety: What Are Seat Belts Used For?

Experiment/Demonstration #171

Procedure:

Place a doll or other small object on a roller skate or small wagon and lay a brick or similar heavy object in its path. Push the skate so that it rolls along the desk top or floor and hits the brick. Note what happens to the doll when the skate is stopped.

Tie the doll to the skate and repeat the experiment. Note that there is now little or no forward movement of the doll when the skate stops.

Materials Needed:

Doll   Brick   Roller Skate   String

How Can We Make a Parachute?

Experiment/Demonstration #172

Procedure:

Tie a string about eight inches long to each corner of a large handkerchief. Fasten some lightweight object, such as a thread spool, to the strings. Wrap the handkerchief and strings around the spool and throw it up in the air. As it falls, the parachute will open and slow the fall of the spool. It may be necessary to increase or decrease the weight to make the parachute open properly.

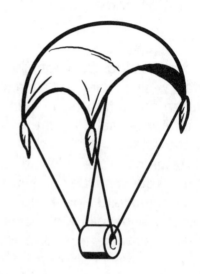

Materials Needed:

Handkerchief   String   Spool

Artificial Satellites: What Is Meant by Centrifugal Force?

Experiment/Demonstration #173

Procedure:

Students ask many questions about why artificial satellites continue to revolve about the earth. The demonstration in the diagram should provide the basis for an understanding of this problem. Tie a stout cord, several feet in length, to a one-hole rubber stopper. Run the other end of the cord through another rubber stopper. Holding the second stopper in one hand, swing the stopper at the end of the string in a wide circle to represent the revolution of the Moon about the earth. What does the pull on the cord represent? The outward pull? How does the Moon continue to revolve about the earth? What happens when the stopper is swinging in a wide circle and the cord is pulled quickly to shorten its orbit?

Materials Needed:

Stout Cord   Two One-hole Stoppers

98

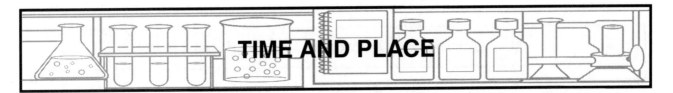

TIME AND PLACE

While the questions When? and Where? may seem simple to answer, it can be challenging for students to deal with different time zones, latitude and longitude, directions, and maps. The experiments and demonstrations in this section will help students understand why there are time zones, the principles behind the latitude and longitude grid on the globe, and how to read and create maps.

Questions explored in this section include:

- How should we approach the study of time?
- What are some devices for keeping time?
- Upon what does the period of a pendulum depend?
- What are the time zones in the United States?
- How can we make a time cone?
- What is meant by latitude and longitude?
- How can we show that the angular distance of the North Star above the horizon equals the latitude?
- How can we use a sextant to measure latitude?
- How can we make a sextant?
- How can we make a map?
- How can we make a contour model?
- How can we use the scale of distances?
- How can we use a topographic map?

How Should We Approach the Study of Time?

Experiment/Demonstration #174

Procedure:

The study of time can be approached in an interesting way by showing how the ability to estimate time varies. Divide the class into two groups and ask one group to sit quietly with their eyes closed and to raise their hands at the end of two minutes. Members of the other group can observe the variation in the estimates. Repeat the procedure with the groups interchanged.

Discuss ways of estimating time, using pulse rate or respiration rate, and repeat the procedure after pupils have recognized the need for using some rhythmic procedure, such as counting seconds by saying "one-thousand and one," "one thousand and two," etc.

What Are Some Devices for Keeping Time?

Experiment/Demonstration #175

Procedure:

Demonstrate some of the devices for measuring time. An egg timer uses the same principle as the hourglass. Similar water clocks can easily be made. Some pupils may be interested in making various types of sundials. Use a string and weight to make a pendulum that beats seconds. A pendulum 99.3 centimeters in length from the point of suspension to the center of the weight will require one second to swing in each direction. It will therefore have a period of two seconds.

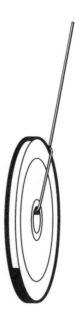

Materials Needed:

Weight(s)   String   Ring Stand

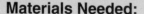

Upon What Does the Period of a Pendulum Depend?

Experiment/Demonstration #176

Procedure:

Use the procedure shown in the diagram to demonstrate that the period depends on the length of the pendulum but not on the weight. Raise the pendulum while it is swinging by pulling on the string. Try different sized weights. Suspend a weight by means of a fine steel wire as shown in the diagrams at the left. Rotate the weight and release it. Torsion clocks operate on this principle. Examine the hairspring and escapement in a watch or alarm clock. Point out that a little of the energy stored up in the mainspring is imparted to the escapement every time the clock ticks.

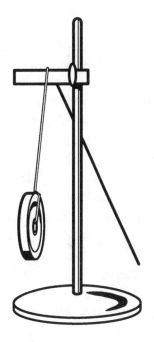

Materials Needed:

Weight	Fine Steel Wire
Ring Stand	Watch or Alarm Clock

What Are the Time Zones in the United States?

Experiment/Demonstration #177

Procedure:

On a map of the United States showing the standard time zones, locate the meridians that determine the standard time used in each zone. Discuss the reasons why time zones are necessary and why the borders are very irregular. Ask students to give examples of radio and television programs that illustrate time differences across the country. Make a diagram explaining how the time zones shift when daylight savings time is used.

How Can We Make a Time Cone?

Experiment/Demonstration #178

Procedure:

Make a time cone that will sit on a globe with the base on the parallel of latitude of your community. First, draw a circle on a piece of heavy paper. After cutting out the disk, cut it along a radius. Overlap one edge to form a cone as shown in the diagram. Adjust the circumference of the base of the cone so it rests on the earth approximately on the 42° parallel. Close the cone with a paper clip and put a mark on the base for each of the 15° meridians. Open up the cone and number the meridians in a counterclockwise direction as shown in the diagram. Then form the cone again and place it on the globe.

Select 8 or 10 places around the earth and observe the time for each. Set the cone on the globe so that the local time is on the 75° meridian. Point out that most of the world's time zones are centered on the meridians that are divisible by 15, such as 75, 105, and 135.

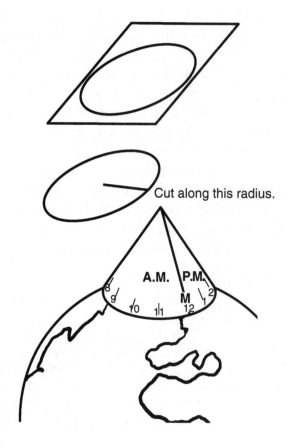

Cut along this radius.

Materials Needed:

Heavy Paper   Scissors
Thin Marker   Globe
Paper Clip

What Is Meant by Latitude and Longitude?

Experiment/Demonstration #179

Procedure:

Many students have erroneous concepts of the meaning of latitude and longitude, largely because of the repeated definition of these terms as "distances" on the surface of the earth. The simple model in the accompanying diagram may be used to show how the location of the meridians and the parallels is determined by angles at the center of the earth.

Make a ball of modeling clay two or three inches in diameter. The ball can be made spherical by rolling it on a smooth surface with the palm of the hand. Cut out a quarter-section as shown at *a*. On an index card, draw a circle of the same diameter as the ball. Measure off angles of 10 or 15 degrees with a protractor and cut out the disk *b*. Fold the disk along a diameter and fit it in the cutout portion of the ball as shown at *c*. Mark the meridians and parallels on the ball in the positions determined by the points where the sides of the angles meet the surface of the sphere as shown in *d*. These lines can easily be marked in the modeling clay with a paper clip.

Relate the arc on the surface to the central angle. Point out how the distance in miles per degree of longitude varies from a maximum of 69.65 miles at the equator to zero at the poles. Some students will be interested in variations in the distance in miles per degree of latitude because of the flattened shape of the earth. At the equator a degree of latitude is equal to about 68.7 miles; at the poles it is about 69.4 miles.

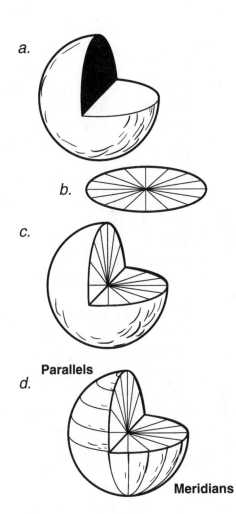

a.

b.

c.

Parallels

d.

Meridians

Materials Needed:

Modeling Clay
Scissors
Pen or Marker

Index Card
Protractor
Paper Clips

How Can We Show That the Angular Distance of the North Star Above the Horizon Equals the Latitude?

Experiment/Demonstration #180

Procedure:

Lay two 12-inch rulers end to end and fasten them together with a piece of transparent tape to form a hinge. This hinge can be used to show that the angular distance of the North Star above the horizon equals the latitude at any point in the Northern Hemisphere.

Press the joint of the hinge against the globe at any point so that one of the rulers points in the direction of the North Star. Point out that the other ruler represents the horizon line. When the hinge is held against the equator, both rulers point in the same direction and the latitude is obviously zero. As the hinge is moved northward on the globe the rulers diverge more and more until they form an angle of 90° at the North Pole as shown in the diagram. Press the hinge against the globe at the latitude of New York state. Holding the rulers in this position, take them away and measure the angle with a protractor. A crude reading of this kind cannot be too accurate, but it will be close to that of the latitude of New York state.

Call attention to the fact that the angle of divergence of the rulers is always equal to the angle formed at the center of the earth by two lines dropped from the equator and the point at which the hinge is held.

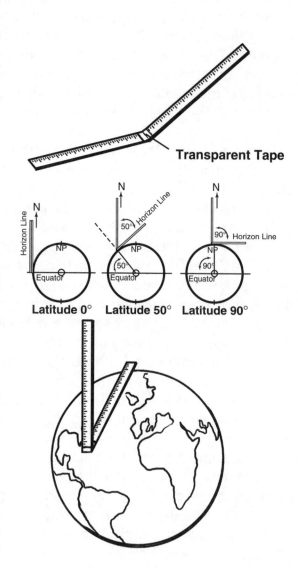

Latitude 0°   **Latitude 50°**   **Latitude 90°**

Materials Needed:

Two Rulers   Heavy (clear) Tape
Globe   Protractor

How Can We Use a Sextant to Measure Latitude?

Experiment/Demonstration #181

Procedure:

Students can measure the latitude by direct observation of the North Star with a sextant.

Make the simple sextant shown in the diagram and sight along the top of the stick to the North Star. When the North Star is in line with the stick, press the thumb and finger over the thread and protractor to hold it in position. The latitude can then be read directly from the scale with a flashlight or match for illumination.

Demonstrate the sextant in the classroom by showing where the plumb line would fall if the observation were made at the equator and at the North Pole.

Sextants like those used for navigation can be inexpensive. This type can be used to determine latitude by "shooting the Sun."

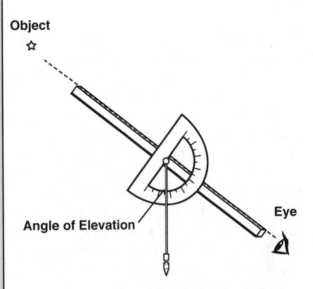

Materials Needed:

Thumbtack   Cardboard Protractor
Straight Stick   Thread
Nail

How Can We Make a Sextant?

Experiment/Demonstration #182

Procedure:

A simple device that can be used both as a sextant and as a transit is shown in the diagram. One or more students may wish to construct one as a project.

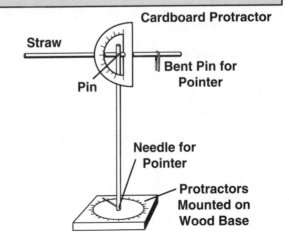

How Can We Make a Map?

Experiment/Demonstration #183

Procedure:

Mapmaking is easy and interesting after a few of the elementary principles are understood. To begin, select any relatively small and level area such as the school lawn. Then place a drawing board or similar flat board on a box or stool and drive a short stake beneath it. Place a magnetic compass on the edge of the paper tacked to the drawing board and turn the mapping board until the compass needle is parallel with the edge of the paper. Draw and label the north-south line. Place a dot near the center of the sheet of paper. This dot represents the position of the mapping board. Use a three-cornered ruler or a straight stick as a sighting vane. Making certain that the sighting edge of the vane remains on the dot, sight each of the objects along the edge of the vane and draw lines from the dot toward the objects. Using a tape, measure the distance from the stake beneath the mapping board to each of the objects sighted. If desired, the distances may be paced off instead of measured. From the dot near the center of the paper, lay off to a suitable scale the distances from the mapping board to the various objects. The result should be a reasonably accurate scale map of the area.

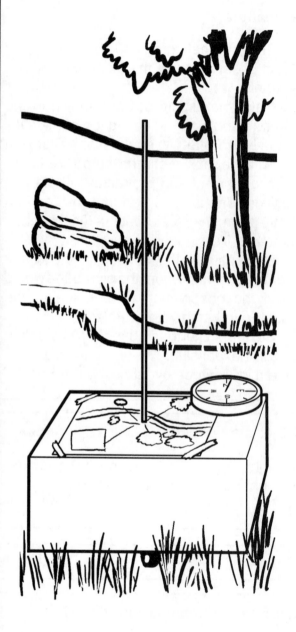

Materials Needed:

Drawing Board	Large Piece of Paper
Pen/Pencil	Magnetic Compass
Stool	Stake
Three-Cornered Ruler/Straight Stick	

Experiment/Demonstration #184

Procedure:

Information sufficient to make a good map may be obtained with no more equipment than two legs, a pencil, and a piece of paper. Pace off the distances between any three objects and jot down these distances on a rough sketch of a triangle. Pace off distances to any other objects desired on the map and indicate them on additional triangles.

After these distances have been recorded, decide upon an appropriate scale for the map. Draw a line to represent the first scale distance on the map paper. Measure off the second scale distance on a ruler with a pair of dividers. Place the point of the dividers on the end of the line and draw an arc. Now measure off the third distance and draw another arc that cuts across the first one. When the intersection of the two arcs is connected with the ends of the line, the resulting triangle will be in the right scale. The map may be enlarged by adding additional triangles.

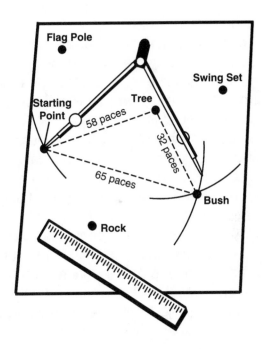

Materials Needed:

Pencil
Piece of Paper
Ruler
Pair of Dividers

107

Experiment/Demonstration #185

Procedure:

Distant and inaccessible points to be mapped present problems. The following example illustrates the principle used in the mapping of large areas.

Drive two stakes 100 feet apart on the school grounds to serve as the ends of a line called the baseline. Set a stool or other support at one end of the baseline, and upon it place a compass or sextant.

Select a distant object and measure the number of degrees between the baseline and the line of sight to the object. Now move to the other end of the baseline and take a similar reading.

Draw the baseline to a convenient scale on the drawing paper and indicate the compass bearing in one corner. Place a protractor on the baseline and measure off the angles to the object observed at each end. Extend these lines until they meet. The point where the two lines meet will be the scale position of the object on the map. As many additional points as desired may be located on the map in a similar way.

This procedure illustrates the principle used in the topographic maps prepared by the United States Coast and Geodetic Survey and the United States Geological Survey. Look at one of these maps and find benchmarks, which are indicated by small crosses. The crosses represent the ends of baselines used in making the survey.

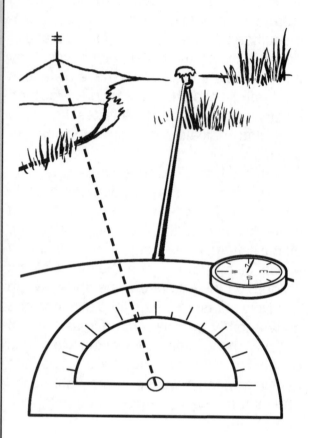

Materials Needed:

Two Stakes Compass/Sextant Protractor
U.S. Coast and Geodetic Survey or
U.S. Geological Survey Maps

How Can We Make a Contour Model?

Experiment/Demonstration #186

Procedure:

The method shown in the diagram represents an interesting approach to contour maps and models. Make a small hill from about one pound of modeling clay and press it into the bottom of a shallow vessel such as a glass jar. Stand a ruler in the pan and pour water into the vessel until it reaches the quarter inch mark. Make a line around the hill at the waterline with a dull pencil. Pour in more water until it reaches another quarter inch and draw another contour. Continue until the contours reach the top of the hill. Pour out the water and remove the hill. The result should be an excellent contour model.

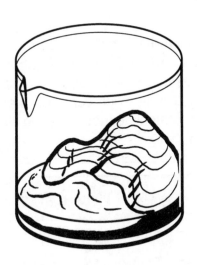

Materials Needed:

Modeling Clay	Glass Jar	Ruler
Dull Pencil	Water	

Experiment/Demonstration #187

Procedure:

A second method of making contour models from modeling clay is shown in the diagram. Form a small hill from modeling clay. Saw some small wooden blocks from a strip of quarter-inch lumber. Lay a file or pencil across one of these blocks and trace a line by moving the blocks and file or pencil around the model hill. Place one block on another and trace a second line, and then a third line and so on. View the "hill" from the top and the two-dimension map effect is apparent. Note the relation of steepness of slope and horizontal distance between lines.

Materials Needed:

Modeling Clay	Wooden Blocks
File or Pencil	

How Can We Use the Scale of Distances?

Experiment/Demonstration #188

Procedure:

Show students how to use the scale of distances. Determine distances to familiar places. Use both airline and road distances. By using the distance scale on maps, students may calculate their traveling distances to school.

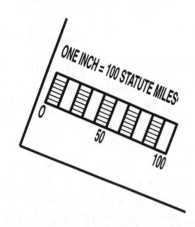

How Can We Use a Topographic Map?

Experiment/Demonstration #189

Procedure:

Students are generally interested in topographic maps because of their scale and because they contain so much familiar detail. In rural areas, they have special significance because every home existing when the map was made has been included. Show students how to orient maps. Place the map flat and turn it until its north-south line as indicated on the map coincides with the north-south line of the locality. The practice of always hanging maps on classroom walls with north at the top results in misunderstanding and confusion. Spend some time picking out well-known features such as lakes, rivers, railroads, and neighboring villages. Discuss the symbols that are used. Look for features that have changed since the area was surveyed. Look for abandoned roads and railroads, burned houses, and new roads and buildings. Call attention to the date of the survey and to other data on the map.

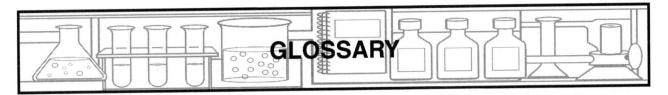

GLOSSARY

A

absorption: taken in; sucked up

ailerons: a pilot-controlled airfoil attached to, in, or near the trailing edge of an airplane wing

air: the elastic invisible mixture of gases (chiefly nitrogen and oxygen, as well as hydrogen, carbon dioxide, argon, neon, helium, etc.) that surrounds the earth

air currents: a vertical movement of air

airplane: a fixed-wing aircraft, heavier than air, that is kept aloft by the aerodynamic forces of air as it is driven forward by a screw propeller or by other means, such as jet propulsion

altostratus: the type of gray or bluish cloud found at intermediate altitudes and consisting of a thick, dense, extensive layer of ice crystals and water droplets

alum: a double sulfate of a monovalent metal or radical with a trivalent metal; used as an astringent, as an emetic, and in the manufacture of baking powders, dyes, and paper

anemometer: a gauge for determining the force or speed of the wind, and sometimes its direction

anticline: a sharply arched fold of stratified rock from whose central axis the strata slope downward in opposite directions

apparatus: the instruments, materials, tools, etc. needed for a specific use

aquarium: a tank, usually with glass sides, or a pool or bowl, etc. for keeping live water animals and water plants

armature: a framework for supporting clay or other material in modeling

artesian well: a well drilled deep enough to reach water that is draining down from higher surrounding ground above the well so that the pressure will force a flow of water upward

artificial satellite: man-made object put into orbit around a planet or a moon

atmosphere: the gaseous envelope (air) surrounding the earth to a height of 621 miles

atmospheric pressure: the pressure due to the weight of the earth's atmosphere; one standard atmosphere equals 14.69 pounds per square inch of pressure and measures 29.92 inches in a barometer of mercury

B

balancing point: the point at which an object's weight is divided equally

barometer: an instrument for measuring atmospheric pressure, especially an aneroid barometer or an evacuated and graduated glass tube (mercury barometer); barometers are used in forecasting changes in the weather or finding height above sea level

barometric pressure: the pressure of the atmosphere as indicated by a barometer

baseline: a horizontal line measured with special accuracy to provide a base for survey by triangulation

beaker: a jarlike container of glass or metal with a lip for pouring, used by chemists

benchmarks: surveyor's marks made on a permanent landmark of known position and altitude: it is used for a reference point in determining other values

bimetal (bimetallic): of, containing, or using two metals, often two metals bonded together

bimetal thermal strip: two metals bonded together, usually brass and steel, with different heat expansion rates

blotting paper: a thick absorbent paper used to dry a surface that has just been written on with ink

bulb: the temperature-sensitive spherical tip of a thermometer

Bunsen burner: a small gas burner that produces a hot, blue flame, used in science laboratories; it consists of a hollow metal tube with holes at the bottom for admitting air to be mixed with gas

C

calibrate: to fix, correct, or check the graduations of (a measuring instrument, as a thermometer)

capillary action: upper movement of liquid through soil

centrifugal force: an apparent force tending to pull a thing outward when it is rotating around a center

circumference: the line bounding a circle, a rounded surface, or an area suggesting a circle

cirrocumulus: the type of white cloud resembling a small puff, flake, or streak, found at high altitudes and consisting of ice crystals and water droplets; mackerel sky

cirrostratus: the type of thin, whitish clouds; such clouds often produce the halo phenomenon

cirrus: the type of cloud resembling a wispy filament, found at high altitudes and consisting of ice crystals

cloud: a visible mass of tiny, condensed water droplets or ice crystals suspended in the atmosphere

coagulate: to cause to curdle; to cause (a liquid) to become a soft, semisolid mass

compass: any of various instruments for showing direction, especially one consisting of a magnetic needle swinging freely on a pivot and pointing to the magnetic north

condensation: the act of condensing, as the reduction of a gas to a liquid

conductor: a substance or thing that is a channel of heat, electricity, sound, etc.

conservation: the act or practice of protecting from loss, waste, etc.; preservation

contour map: a map showing contour lines with equal elevations along each separate line

contraction: reduction in size, drawn together, shrink, narrow, shorten

convection current: the transfer of heat by means of current

convex surface: curved outward like the surface of a sphere

copper shot: small pellets made of copper

crystal: a clear transparent quartz

cumulonimbus: the type of dense cloud developing vertically through all cloud levels, consisting of water droplets, ice crystals, and sometimes hail, and associated with thunder, lightning and heavy showers

cumulus: the type of bright, billowy cloud developing vertically through all cloud levels, with a dark, flat base, and consisting mostly of water droplets

D

debris: rough broken bits and pieces of stone, wood, glass, etc.

delta: a deposit of sand and soil, usually triangular, formed at the mouth of a river

dew: the condensation formed, usually during the night, on lawns, cars, etc., as a result of warm air contacting a cool surface

distill: to purify or refine

drag: a resisting force exerted on an aircraft parallel to its airstream and opposite in direction to its motion

dry ice: carbon dioxide solidified and compressed into snowlike cakes that vaporize at -78.5°C without passing through a liquid state; used as a refrigerant

(sand) dune: a rounded hill or ridge of sand heaped up by the action of the wind

E

egg-timer: a device for measuring time

electric charge: as one body gains positive charge, some other body gains the same amount of negative charge; charges may be produced by rubbing together a variety of materials

electrophorus: an apparatus consisting of an insulated resin disk and a metal plate, used in generating static electricity by induction

elevators: a pilot-controlled airfoil attached to the trailing edge of the tail section's horizontal stabilizers to make an aircraft go up or down and to control pitching

emulsion: a stable colloidal suspension, consisting of an immiscible liquid dispersed and held in another liquid by substances called emulsifiers

Epsom salt: a white crystalline salt, used as a cathartic

erosion: wearing away, disintegrating

escapement: the part in a mechanical clock or watch that controls the speed and regularity of the balance wheel or pendulum, and thereby of the entire mechanism, by the movement of a notched wheel, one tooth of which is permitted to escape from the detaining catch at a time

evaporating dish: open dish with liquid

evaporation: to change a liquid or a solid into vapor; drive out or draw off in the form of a vapor

exhaust: to draw off or let out completely (air, gas, etc.), as from a container, or to use up; to expend completely

expansion: enlargement, dilation

expansion ball & ring: brass ring and ball that may be heated and cooled to show expansion and contraction

F

fault: a fracture or zone of fractures in rock strata together with movement that displaces the sides relative to one another

filter: device for separating solid particles, impurities, etc., from a liquid or a gas by passing it through a porous substance

flask: any small bottle-shaped container with a narrow neck, used in laboratories, etc.

fossil: any hardened remains or imprints of plant or animal life of some previous geologic period, preserved in the earth's crust, including petrified wood, resin, etc.

frost: the ice crystals that form directly on freezing surfaces as contacted by moist air

funnel: an instrument consisting of an inverted cone with a hole at the small end, or a tapering or cylindrical tube with a wide, cone-shaped mouth, for pouring liquids and powders into containers with small openings

G

galvanized: to plate metal with zinc, originally by applying electric current

gas: the lightest form of a substance in which it can expand indefinitely to fill its container; form that is neither liquid nor solid

gauge: any device for measuring something, as the thickness of wire, the dimensions of a machined part, the amount of liquid in a container, steam pressure, etc.

glacial deposit: rocks or soil left after a glacier melts or recedes

glacier: a large mass of ice and snow that forms in areas where the rate of snowfall constantly exceeds the rate at which the snow melts: it moves slowly outward from the center of accumulation or down a mountain until it melts or breaks away

graduated cylinder: a cylinder, generally glass, calibrated for measuring

granite: a very hard, crystalline, plutonic rock, gray to pink in color, consisting of feldspar, quartz, and smaller amounts of other minerals

gravel: loose mixture of pebbles and rock fragments coarser than sand, often mixed with clay

H

hairspring: very slender, hairlike coil that controls the regular movement of the balance wheel in a watch or clock

helicopter: a kind of vertical-lift aircraft, capable of hovering or moving in any direction, having a motor-driven, horizontal rotor

hot plate: a small, portable device for cooking food, or heating something, usually with only one or two gas or electric burners

hourglass: an instrument for measuring time by the trickling of sand, mercury, water, etc. through a small opening from one glass bulb to another below it, in a fixed period of time, esp. one hour

humidity: moistness, dampness, the amount or degree of moisture in the air

hygrometer: any of various instruments for measuring the absolute or relative amount of moisture in the air

hypothesis: an unproved theory, proposition, supposition, etc., tentatively accepted to explain certain facts or (working hypothesis) to provide a basis for further investigation, argument, etc.

I

igneous: produced by the action of fire, formed by volcanic action or intense heat, as rocks solidified from molten magma at or below the surface of the earth

J

jet: an airplane propelled by jet propulsion, forcing gas out in a stream

jet propulsion: a method of propelling airplanes, boats, etc., that uses the reaction force created when compressed outside air and hot exhaust gases are forced through a jet nozzle

K

kettle holes: a depression in a glacial drift remaining after the melting of an isolated mass of buried ice

L

lamp wick: a piece of cord, tape, or bundle of threads designed to absorb fuel by capillary action

lath: any of the thin narrow strips of wood used in lattices or nailed to two-by-fours, rafters, etc.

latitude: angular distance measured in degrees, north or south from the equator

lift pump: a suction pump that raises a column of liquid to the level of a spout, out which the liquid runs of its own accord

limestone: rock consisting mainly of calcium carbonate, often composed of the organic remains of sea animals, as mollusks, corals, etc., used as a building stone, a source of lime, etc.; when crystallized by heat and pressure, it becomes marble

liquid: readily flowing; fluid; having its molecules moving freely with respect to each other so as to flow readily, unlike a solid, but because of the cohesive forces not expanding indefinitely like a gas

litmus paper: absorbent paper treated with litmus, used as an acid-base indicator

loam: a rich soil composed of clay, sand, and some organic matter

longitude: distance east or west on the earth's surface, measured as an arc of the equator between the meridian, usually the one passing through Greenwich, England

M

manometer: an instrument for measuring the pressure of gases or liquids

map: a drawing or other representation, usually on a flat surface, of all or part of the earth's surface, ordinarily showing countries, bodies of water, cities, mountains, etc.

meridians: a great circle of the earth passing through the geographical poles and any given point on the surface

metamorphic: of, characterized by, or caused from a change of form, shape structure, or substance; a type of rock formed by the transformation of pre-existing rocks

mineral: an inorganic substance occurring naturally in the earth and having a consistent and distinctive set of physical properties and a composition that can be expressed by a chemical formula

moisture: water or other liquid causing a slight wetness or dampness

N

nimbostratus: the type of extensive gray cloud that obscures the Sun, found at low altitudes and consisting of dense, dark layers of water droplets, rain, or snow

O

orbit: the actual or imaginary path taken by a celestial body during its periodic revolution around another body

oxbow lake: sharp bend in a river that has been dammed at both ends forming a lake

P

parachute: a cloth contrivance usually shaped like an umbrella when expanded, and used to slow the falling speed of a person or thing dropping from an airplane, etc.

paraffin: a white, waxy, odorless, tasteless solid substance consisting of a mixture of straight-chain, saturated hydrocarbons

parallels: any of the imaginary lines parallel to the equator and representing degrees of latitude on the earth's surface

pendulum: an object hung from a fixed point so as to swing freely back and forth under the combined forces of gravity and momentum; often used in regulating the movement of clocks

permeability: the state or quality of being open to passage or penetration

pH: a symbol for the degree of acidity or alkalinity of a solution

pith ball: soft, spongy material, usually from a plant, formed into a ball; very sensitive to electrical charge

place: a particular area or locality; region

plasticene: an oil-base modeling paste, used as a substitute for clay or wax

porous: full of pores, through which fluids, air, or light may pass

precipitation: a depositing of rain, snow, sleet, etc.

propellers: a device on a ship or aircraft consisting typically of two or more blades twisted to describe a helical path as they rotate with the hub in which they are mounted, and serving to propel the craft by the backward thrust of air or water

R

radiation: the process in which energy in the form of rays of light, heat, etc., is sent out through space from atoms and molecules as they go through internal changes

radius: any straight line extending from the center to the periphery (outside) of a circle or sphere

rate: the amount, degree, etc., of anything in relation to units of something else (*rate* of speed per hour)

relative humidity: the amount of moisture in the air as compared with the maximum amount that the air could contain at the same temperature, expressed as a percentage

relief map: a map showing by color, raised areas, etc., the different heights of land forms, such as hills and valleys

reservoirs: places where anything is collected and stored, generally in large quantities; especially a natural or artificial lake or pond in which water is collected and stored for use

ring stand: metal upright for clamping scientific equipment in some science experiments

rock: mineral matter variously composed, formed in masses or large quantities in the earth's crust by the action of heat, water, etc.

rocket: any of various devices, typically cylindrical, containing liquid or solid propellants, which when ignited produce hot gases or ions that escape through a rear vent and drive the container forward by the principle of reaction

rubber tubing: a slender pipe made of rubber used for conveying fluids

rudder: broad flat movable piece of wood or metal hinged vertically at the stern of a boat or ship, used for steering

runoff: something that runs off, as rain in excess of the amount absorbed by the ground

S

sandstone: a common bedded sedimentary rock much used for building, composed largely of sand grains, mainly quartz, held together by silica lime, etc.

satellite: a moon traveling around a larger planet, a man made object rocketed into orbit around Earth, the Moon, etc.

saturated: filled to capacity; having absorbed all that can be taken up

scale model: the proportion that a map, model, etc., bears to the thing that it represents

sealing wax: combination of resin and turpentine used for sealing letters, dry cells, etc.; it is hard at normal temperatures, but softens when heated

sediment: matter that settles to the bottom of a liquid; matter deposited by water or wind

sedimentary: containing sediment, formed by the deposit of sediment

seed: provides a partial nucleus around which water vapor forms

sextant: an instrument used by navigators for measuring the angular distance of the Sun, a star, etc. from the horizon, as in finding the position of a ship

shale: a kind of fine-grained, thinly-bedded sedimentary rock formed largely by the hardening of clay; it splits easily into thin layers

shallow: not deep

siphon: bent tube used for carrying liquid from a reservoir over the top of the edge of its container to a point below the surface of the reservoir; the tube must be filled, as by suction, before flow will start

slate: a hard, fine-grained, metamorphic rock that cleaves naturally into thin, smooth-surfaced layers

smoke paper: burned paper still emitting smoke

soil: the surface layer of the earth, supporting plant life

solder wire: a metal alloy used when melted for joining or patching metal parts or surfaces

solid: tending to keep its form rather than to flow or spread out like a liquid or gas; relatively firm or compact

stalactite: an icicle-shaped, secondary mineral deposit that hangs from the roof in a cave and is formed by the evaporation of water that is full of minerals

stalagmite: a cone-shaped, secondary mineral deposit built up on the floor of a cave by dripping materials

stratocumulus: the type of white or gray cloud found at low altitudes and consisting of large, smooth or patchy layers of water droplets and possibly some hail or snow

stratum: a horizontal layer or section of material, especially any of several lying one upon another

stratus: type of gray cloud found at low altitudes and consisting of a uniform layer of water droplets and sometimes ice crystals

sundial: an instrument that indicates time by the position of a gnomon's shadow cast by the Sun on the face of a dial marked in hours

supersaturated: to make more highly concentrated than in normal saturation at a given temperature

synclines: a down fold in stratified rocks from whose central axis the beds rise upward and outward in opposite directions

T

temperature: the degree of hotness or coldness of anything, usually as measured on a thermometer

terrarium: an enclosure, such as a glass tank, in which to keep small land animals

test tube: a tube of thin, transparent glass closed at one end, used in chemical experiments, etc.

thermal: having to do with heat

thermometer: an instrument for measuring temperatures, consisting of a graduated glass tube with a sealed, capillary bore in which mercury, colored alcohol, etc. rises or falls as it expands or contracts from changes in temperature

thermostat: an apparatus for regulating temperature, esp. one that automatically controls a heating or cooling unit

thistle tube: a thistle-shaped glass tube used to move liquids in science experiments, has various uses

thrust: to push with sudden force; drive

time: indefinite, unlimited duration in which things are considered as happening in the past, present, or future

time cone: calibrated cone placed over globe at north pole showing time zones

tongs: a device for seizing or lifting objects, having two long arms pivoted or hinged together

topographic: the science of drawing on maps and charts or otherwise representing the surface features of a region, including its relief and rivers, lakes, etc. and such man-made features as canals and bridges, roads, and so on

topographic map: a map representing the surface features of a region including its relief, rivers, lakes, etc.

topsoil: the upper layer of soil, usually darker and richer than the subsoil; surface soil

tumbler: an ordinary drinking glass without foot or stem

V

vacuum pump: pump used to draw air out of sealed space

vessel: a utensil for holding something, as a vase, bowl, pot, kettle, etc.

W

water table: the level below which the ground is saturated with water

water vapor: water in the form of gas; steam

weather: general condition of the atmosphere at a particular time and place, with regard to the temperature, moisture, cloudiness, and so on

weather vane: a vane that swings in the wind to show the direction from which the wind is blowing

wind: air in motion; specifically any noticeable natural movement of air parallel to the earth's surface

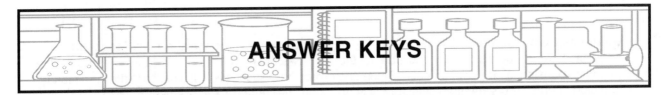

ANSWER KEYS

Experiment/Demonstration #1 (page 9)

The egg will drop into the bottle in a matter of seconds. The flame "uses up" most of the oxygen in the milk bottle. Since there is then less pressure pushing upward, and more pressure pushing downward, the egg is literally "pushed" into the bottle.

Experiment/Demonstration #2 (page 9)

Atmospheric pressure will collapse the can.

Experiment/Demonstration #3 (page 10)

Atmospheric pressure will collapse the can since the pressure is greater on the outside of the can.

Experiment/Demonstration #4 (page 10)

The card will "stick" to the top of the glass. The upward push of the air kept the card and water in place. Simply stated, the water "drove" most of the air out of the glass. The force pressing against the card was greater—had more strength—than the air pressure contained in the water-filled glass.

Experiment/Demonstration #5 (page 11)

The water does not run out of the glass because of the atmospheric pressure on the surface of the water in the vessel.

Experiment/Demonstration #6 (page 11)

When you try to pull them apart, you may find this to be very difficult because practically all of the air has been forced out of the inside portion of the suction cups. Consequently, the outsides of the cups have more air pressing on them than the insides of the cups.

Experiment/Demonstration #7 (page 12)

Water will stop flowing from the hole. Lift your hand and water will start to flow again.

Experiment/Demonstration #8 (page 12)

The water will be expelled from the carton and the "submarine" will float. Air pressure inside the balloon forces the water out of the "submerged submarine."

Experiment/Demonstration #9 (page 13)

You won't be able to drink because of the lack of air pressure from outside the bottle.

Experiment/Demonstration #10 (page 13)

When the stopper is loosened, it allows outside air pressure to enable you to drink water.

Experiment/Demonstration #11 (page 14)

The pressure of the atmosphere on the surface of the water in the dish keeps the water from running out of the jar.

Experiment/Demonstration #12 (page 14)

Lack of air pressure causes the stopper to "stick" to the surface.

Experiment/Demonstration #13 (page 15)

The dropper fills because the rubber bulb is elastic and tends to resume its original shape after being squeezed. Atmospheric pressure on the surface of the water in the vessel forces water into the dropper.

Experiment/Demonstration #14 (page 15)

Atmospheric pressure on the water surfaces of both vessels keeps the siphon filled with water. When the two connected vessels are on the same level no water flows because the pressure is the same on each side. Raising one vessel increases the length of the column of water in the siphon on the side of the second vessel. Consequently, the pressure of the column of water in the siphon is now greater on the side of the second vessel, and the water flows until the columns are again the same length.

Experiment/Demonstration #19 (page 19)

Applying heat energy to metals causes them to expand, therefore letting the ball pass.

Experiment/Demonstration #20 (page 19)

When copper wire is heated, it will expand, causing the weight to slowly drop to the table and stop swinging freely. When the wire is cooled it will contract to its original length.

Experiment/Demonstration #21 (page 20)

Heat caused the wire to expand and drop the weight closer to the table. As the wire cooled, it contracted to its original length.

Experiment/Demonstration #22 (page 20)

The wires sag because heating them causes them to expand. One wire will sag more than the other.

Experiment/Demonstration #23 (page 21)

When heated, the strip will bend due to the unequal expansion of the two metals. Since the expansion of brass is greater than steel, brass is on the outside of the band.

Experiment/Demonstration #25 (page 22)

When heated, copper expands more than tin; this causes one end to bend when the other end is clamped in a fixed position.

Experiment/Demonstration #26 (page 22)

During the cold temperatures of the winter, the tiny molecules of water in sidewalks and roads freeze and expand, then warm and contract depending on temperatures. If the roads and sidewalks aren't in sections with spaces left for the expansion, cracks and holes can appear.

When metal is warmed or heated, it also expands, making a metal lid looser on a jar, therefore easier to remove.

When air is trapped within tires and is heated, causing the air to expand, tires can become overfilled, and it is more likely for a blowout to occur if some air is not released.

Experiment/Demonstration #27 (page 23)

Heating expands the liquid and it rises into the tube. Cooling contracts the liquid, causing its level to fall.

Experiment/Demonstration #28 (page 23)

When one flask is heated, the air expands, driving some of the air out of the flask. The air in the heated flask will then weigh less than the air in the unheated flask, causing the two flasks to be unbalanced—the heated one moving up, the unheated moving down.

Experiment/Demonstration #29 (page 24)

If the air in the flask is heated, the air will be driven out. When the air in the flask has time to cool, some of the colored water will rise into the glass tube.

Experiment/Demonstration #30 (page 24)

The heated air that is driven from the flask is pushed into the balloon, blowing the balloon up.

Experiment/Demonstration #31 (page 25)

The coated tube has a higher temperature.

Experiment/Demonstration #32 (page 25)

As the heat travels along the wire, the shot will drop off in succession. If allowed to drop in a metal pie pan, the impact as a shot strikes the pan can easily be heard.

Experiment/Demonstration #33 (page 26)

Region A will boil, but region B will remain cold. The test tube could be held with your hand in region B, while region A is boiling. This shows that both water and glass are poor conductors of heat.

Experiment/Demonstration #34 (page 26)

The ice will melt slowly. The top part of the tube will gradually get hot. The wire could get warm depending on the amount of time to melt the size of the ice cube.

Experiment/Demonstration #35 (page 27)

The sawdust moves in current streams.

Experiment/Demonstration #36 (page 27)

The colored water moves through the glass tube, showing convection currents.

Experiment/Demonstration #37 (page 28)

The smoke moves from one chimney through the other, showing wind currents.

Experiment/Demonstration #38 (page 28)

The smoke moves in air currents, showing convection currents.

Experiment/Demonstration #39 (page 29)

The spiral rotates, showing convection currents of air.

Experiment/Demonstration #40 (page 29)

The wheel turns, showing the convection currents of air.

Experiment/Demonstration #42 (page 30)

The column rises when heated and falls when cooled.

Experiment/Demonstration #47 (page 33)

As water evaporates from the cloth it weighs less, upsetting the balance of the stick.

Experiment/Demonstration #48 (page 34)

As water evaporates from the soil, it weighs less, therefore the balance is upset.

Experiment/Demonstration #49 (page 34)

Transpiration causes water droplets to form on the inside of the plastic wrap.

Experiment/Demonstration #50 (page 34)

If the humidity is not too low, moisture will collect on the can. On a very dry day there may be too little water vapor in the air for any to condense on the cold surface of the can. If this happens set the can of water and ice in a large beaker with a moist sponge or towel in the bottom and cover the beaker with a pane of glass.

Experiment/Demonstration #51 (page 35)

When warm, moist air is cooled, water drops appear, and when reheated, the moisture evaporates.

Experiment/Demonstration #52 (page 35)

The water will evaporate more quickly from the vessel that has more surface area. The large surface area allows for more interaction between the water and air, causing more evaporation.

Experiment/Demonstration #53 (page 36)

More water will evaporate from the jar that is warmer because there is more molecular activity when the water is heated.

Experiment/Demonstration #55 (page 37)

The alcohol evaporates. The temperature of the hand decreases.

Experiment/Demonstration #57 (page 38)

The dewpoint is determined by the individual place where the experiment takes place—the temperature when dew is formed.

Experiment/Demonstration #66 (page 42)

The color will vary with the amount of moisture in the air.

Experiment/Demonstration #67 (page 42)

The amount of water in each sample of snow will vary depending on whether the snow is "wet" or "dry."

Experiment/Demonstration #69 (page 43)

Blowing in the jar raises relative humidity, and with the smoke inside, the conditions are perfect for condensation. When pressure is suddenly released, smog appears. When the jar is blown into again, the smog disappears, just as the smog will reappear if pressure is suddenly released again.

Experiment/Demonstration #70 (page 44)

Fog forms in the bottle with hot water because of the hot and cold air meeting. There is no fog in the bottle with cold water because there is not enough temperature difference between the cold water and the ice cube.

Experiment/Demonstration #74 (page 46)

Raindrops freeze as they pass through cold layers of air in the container and in the air on the way to the earth.

Experiment/Demonstration #75 (page 46)

Soil heats and cools more rapidly than water.

Experiment/Demonstration #76 (page 47)

Water in the white can should be the coolest, and the water in the black can should be the warmest.

Experiment/Demonstration #77 (page 47)

The water in the test tube that has been colored with marker should be the hottest.

Experiment/Demonstration #85 (page 53)

The sharp edges have been rounded and worn away.

Experiment/Demonstration #94 (page 58)

Roots of the bean seeds start to penetrate the plaster, causing the plaster to crack or to scale off.

Experiment/Demonstration #96 (page 59)

The freezing water will expand and break the jar. Absorbed water often breaks rocks in the same manner.

Experiment/Demonstration #97 (page 59)

It gains weight as it is soaking. If frozen, it will likely break.

Experiment/Demonstration #99 (page 60)

The unprotected soil is washed and splashed away, whereas the soil forms columns under the coins.

Experiment/Demonstration #104 (page 62)

Erosion occurs differently in each metal pan, depending on the protection from rain.

Experiment/Demonstration #107 (page 63)

The lighter and smaller pieces are suspended the longest, making them the easiest to get carried away.

Experiment/Demonstration #111 (page 65)
Ice cubes pick up soil particles, and when they slide downhill and melt, the soil is deposited where they melt.

Experiment/Demonstration #123 (page 70)
a) The one with loose soil loses the most soil.
b) The soil without sod loses the most soil.
c) The tray with the most slope loses the most soil.

Experiment/Demonstration #131 (page 76)
The water pressure increases as the thistle tube goes deeper under water.

Experiment/Demonstration #135 (page 78)
The looser the soil, the faster the water goes into the soil.

Experiment/Demonstration #149 (page 84)
Water mixed with detergent makes the "dirt" break up more rapidly.

Experiment/Demonstration #153 (page 87)
The moving air lessens air pressure as it rolls over the curved surface.

Experiment/Demonstration #154 (page 88)
Lift occurs, and the platform balance becomes unbalanced because of the change in air pressure.

Experiment/Demonstration #155 (page 88)
The air moves in one direction while the fan is moving in the opposite direction.

Experiment/Demonstration #156 (page 89)
The paper sticks straight out because the fast air above is low pressure, and the slow high pressure below keeps it straight out.

Experiment/Demonstration #157 (page 89)
The flame goes toward the card because as the air goes around it, the air becomes turbulent, which slows and turns the flow.

Experiment/Demonstration #158 (page 90)
Air currents move smoothly around the streamlined cardboard, pushing the flame outwards.

Experiment/Demonstration #162 (page 92)
The cork "pops" out of the bottle because the alcohol expands.

Experiment/Demonstration #163 (page 92)
Gas forces the cork from the bottle. The gas and bottle go different directions

Experiment/Demonstration #164 (page 93)
A jet of water through the tube shows thrust.

Experiment/Demonstration #165 (page 93)
The thrust of escaping water revolves the can like a rotary lawn sprinkler.

Experiment/Demonstration #173 (page 98)
1. The pull on the cord represents gravity.
2. The outward pull on the cord represents centrifugal force.
3. The Moon continues to revolve about the earth because its own inertia keeps it in motion and because the two forces exactly balance each other.
4. The stopper moves more rapidly when the orbit is shortened.
The nearer a satellite is to the earth, the greater the pull of gravity. Artificial satellites must travel with tremendous speed to have enough centrifugal force to balance the pull of gravity upon them.

Acknowledgement: The Illinois Department of Education